Islam, Multiculturalism and Transnationalism

ISLAM, MULTICULTURALISM and TRANSNATIONALISM

From the Lebanese Diaspora

Michael Humphrey

The Centre for Lebanese Studies
in association with
I.B.Tauris Publishers
London • New York

Published in 1998 by
The Centre for Lebanese Studies, Oxford
in association with
I.B. Tauris & Co Ltd
Victoria House
Bloomsbury Square
London WC1B 4DZ

175 Fifth Avenue
New York NY 10010

In the United States of America
and in Canada distributed by
St Martin's Press
175 Fifth Avenue
New York NY 10010

A full CIP record for this book is available from the British Library
A full CIP record for this book is available from the Library of Congress

ISBN 1 86064 356 6

Library of Congress catalog card number: available

Typeset in Minion by Hepton Books, Oxford
Printed and bound in Great Britain by Biddles Ltd, Guildford and King's Lynn

Contents

Acknowledgements

I would like to thank the many people who at different times and in different ways have contributed to the writing of this book. Foremost is the generosity and engagement of many Lebanese who gave me their attention and time so that I could become a better student of their experiences and history in Lebanon and Australia. In this regard I would particularly like to acknowledge the Lebanese Muslim communities in Sydney who were the main focus of this study.

I would especially like to thank Professor Michael Gilsenan for his commentary on early manuscripts, Nadim Shehadi, Director of the Centre for Lebanese Studies in Oxford for his support in publishing, and Anna Enayat for her editorial skill in polishing the manuscript.

I would also like to acknowledge the contributions over the years of Abdallah Mograby, Bob Springborg and Andrew Vincent to my understanding of Middle Eastern worlds and cultural life.

Without the support and encouragement of my wife, Estela and daughters, Lucy and Cecilia, this book would have been even harder to complete.

Michael Humphrey
February 1998

1

Local and Global Cultures

This study is about migration, social membership, and social attachment. Its concern is the mobility of individuals between the South and the North and the forms of attachment that exist in an increasingly plural world. Migration is often used as a natural metaphor for modernity, the progress of individual lives from the traditional to the modern; but in the contemporary world the journey is not one way. People do not leave one world behind and become enclosed in another through work (proletarianised) or becoming new citizens (nationalised). The places of belonging – households, communities, cities and nations – are becoming more unstable through the impact of global economic uncertainties, political crises and pluralisation. More and more people are living between different places with uncertain futures.

The migration of people is increasingly about the internationalisation of societies rather than the cultural or class homogenisation of people in nation states. Individuals move from the South to the North for reasons of opportunity, need, fear or to escape the past, both collective and individual. Their individual reasons, however, together constitute the internationalisation of social relations of households, communities and ethnic groups. Families, or parts of families, move from the South to the North thereby making themselves part of an international workforce. By whatever label they are called – migrant, guestworker, illegal worker, refugee – they become members of the growing immigrant working class found in cities of the North.

Their identity in the North is not, however, fashioned by their sameness as wage workers but rather their cultural differences as migrants. Migrants remain attached to others, things, cultures and memories despite the homogenising impetus of proletarianisation and nationalisation. They each have their own project, their plans and hopes; but the act of migration itself is an integral part of the global experience of socialisation into the modern world, of becoming part of urban proletariats, citizens of new and old nations or minorities in national cultures. Migration merely makes the experience of proletarianisation and nationalisation plural rather than singular. Cultural knowledge and memories become the basis for interpreting and knowing new worlds and creating transnational cultural worlds.

The principle site of pluralisation and internationalisation of cultures is the contemporary city. Living cheek by jowl in the cities of the North, the new immigrant proletariat discovers its cultural identity as relational. People who had never been in close proximity elaborate knowledge about the Other through cultural difference. The same processes are at work in rural–urban migration in the South. The plurality of regional or local identities are given new significance when they are brought together in the city and become the basis of new identities. The experience of proletarianisation through migration to the city forms around solidarities of community in neighbourhoods rather than solidarities of labour in the workplace.

Cultural identity is not only elaborated in the context of the city but also in the global discourse on relations between the South and North. In the North migrants become a concrete expression of inequality in global relations. They are treated as if they were representatives of other worlds who carry the legacy of their past.

The meaning of difference becomes articulated in post-colonial and Orientalist discourses as well as in local and national discourses. Social position and identity is thus constructed simultaneously within a local and global context – as in the case of Muslim immigrants whose identity is articulated in relation to local ethnic relations as well as to international discourses on Islam.

This book explores the themes of social pluralisation and internationalisation through an anthropological study of Lebanese Muslim immigrants living in Sydney during the period of the Lebanese civil war (1976–90). Its focus is the spatial context of cultural production analysed by looking at the way Lebanese Muslim migrants in Sydney have organised reciprocity in family life, created their households, formed urban communities, become workers, defined sectarian identities, transmitted religious culture through personal networks and institutions and established Islamic institutions.

As a global phenomenon the nation state has been the centrepiece of social incorporation in the modern world, the basis of integration into national culture and class structures. International migration involves relocation from one historically specific experience of incorporation into a nation state to another mediated through the cultural and social worlds of individual migrants. The case of Lebanese Muslim immigrants in Australia provides vivid illustration of this process and an opportunity to explore the relationship of individuals, families and communities to the nation state in the context of the contemporary pluralisation of culture and internationalisation of labour markets. In this respect, the lives of individual immigrants document not so much continuities of cultural practice as the historical experience of incorporation into nation states.

Throughout the book, stories of individual migrants, their biographies and their disputes are interspersed with the text. The first introduces the contemporary Lebanese experience of nation states, international mobility and connections.

Destinies[1]

In June 1990 I met Butrous, a Lebanese Maronite who had just arrived in Sydney having fled the latest round of intra-sectarian fighting in Beirut. Boutrous had managed to secure a tourist visa to visit family members in Australia. His intention was to explore the possibility of continuing his life there.

Fighting continued in his home suburb in Beirut and he managed to extend his stay in Australia on humanitarian grounds. After six months he found there was little prospect of employment in Sydney, especially in his field of English language teaching. Butrous therefore resolved to look at other places where relatives had settled. He decided to try Haiti where a cousin had established a business and where, during his childhood, more than 30 years earlier, he had once lived.

Through his family connections he was able to remain mobile between different destinations in the South and North and to celebrate, through his journey, a belief in his control over his own destiny – or at least his ability to refuse destinies which offered him no future.

The focus on the individual's relationship to the nation state in South–North migration highlights the increasing mobility of populations and the pluralisation of societies. The widespread crisis of the nation state in the South brought about by the failure of economic development, disappointed democratic aspirations and civil war, has undermined the process of national incorporation there. Migration is one expression of that crisis. It connects, through people's lives, the South and the North. The diasporas of the North become conduits for migration as well as a source of remittances to sustain family members in the South.

The transnational structures which sustain the links are more than just family and community networks. The technology) of travel, in person or voice, has collapsed distance as a barrier to participation in the social networks and cultures of the past – an imagined existence in multiple communities and multiple homelands has become possible. There are air-routes, and even national airlines, which depend heavily on the traffic generated by migration – the migrants themselves, visitors, journeys back home, retirements and even burials. The existence of ethnic travel agents is a barometer of the volume of traffic linking different parts of the world. International telecommunication corporations have also profited enormously from the readiness of people to participate in long distance relations by phone, a medium which permits a social presence and continuity.

Nowadays, even the journey to the North is uncertain. The internationalisation of labour, capital and commodity markets is undermining employment security and the scope of state welfare protection. The very idea of settlement, the idea of permanence, is being undermined and so is confidence in the cross-generational social mobility of migrants. Moreover, as cities increasingly become competitive sites for investment and capital, more mobile migrants find themselves the first victims of the hazards of economic recession, political repression, unemployment or racism.[2] Individuals, families and communities learn the contingencies of their acceptance, settlement and integration through the terms of their traditions.

Migrants or Citizens?

In the history of South–North migration, the question of who should be allowed to immigrate has been closely bound up with the idea of who would most easily assimilate. Migration was fundamentally an issue of the preservation of national homogeneity through appropriate selection of migrants, a way to expand and develop nations based on racial and cultural purity.

In white settler societies like Australia, a British dominion society, culture and race were pivotal issues in the formation of the nation state. Cultural exclusiveness carried with it the racist notion that successful nation building depended upon the reconstitution of European society in the periphery. The idea that progress and prosperity depended on the transplantation of European society was perhaps most explicitly formulated by the nineteenth-century Argentine liberal Sarmiento. In his book *Civilisation or Barbarism?* Sarmiento argued that without European migration Argentine society would slip into 'barbarism'.[3] White superiority and racial homogeneity were the common themes in the political consolidation of settler societies as nation states.

The birth of the Australian state (the transition from colony to constitutional monarchy) in 1901 explicitly formulated membership in racial terms. The 'Exclusion Act' denied entry to Asians and Melanesians; its legacy was the 'White Australia' policy which survived well into the post-war era of Australian mass migration – the late 1960s.[4] Indeed the notion that European migration and national development went hand in hand was emphatically restated when the mass migration programme began in 1947 by the minister of immigration, Arthur Calwell, whose remarks included the now infamous phrase: 'Two Wongs don't make a White!'

In the 1970s race and culture were gradually eliminated from official discourse on the selection of migrants in the North. The large-scale mobilisation of people internationally produced increasingly plural societies which made assimilation as the official ideology of the nation untenable. In North America and Australia it was replaced by the idea of multiculturalism as official state policy. Multiculturalism prohibited discrimination on the grounds of culture or race in the selection of migrants and their treatment in the host society.

Yet in practice culture and race have remained as markers of social differentiation, if not discrimination. For both are indicators of social position and cultural capital, while the individual act of migration itself, from the perspective of the host society, is still interpreted as a tacit acknowledgement of the superiority of the new over the old society and ways. A recent national inquiry into Australian immigration policy revealed how little the underlying premises of social and political integration had changed. An official report, entitled 'Immigration: a commitment to Australia', suggested that far too many migrants demonstrated their lack of allegiance to Australia by failing to take out citizenship. In the political debate that followed the release of the report it was suggested that immigrants who failed to become naturalised citizens should be penalised by denying them the right to welfare benefits.[5] Proficiency in English language was in addition suggested as a necessary criterion for citizenship – of people who were making the effort to become part of Australian society. Immigration policy sought permanent settlers who would express their gratitude for selection by quickly becoming naturalised Australians and learning English.[6] Becoming part of the same linguistic community was seen as essential for social membership in the Australian national community.

Making social rights contingent on the assumption of political rights (naturalisation) or the acquisition of cultural capital reveals contemporary strategies of incorporation in multicultural nation states. Social membership in the nation state is constituted by different kinds of rights which can be divided into civil, political and social, each with distinct institutional mechanisms for their realisation.[7] Civil rights are associated with individual freedom and secured through law and the court system, political rights allow the participation in the exercise of political power through parliamentary institutions and social rights provide a standard of living through social services and education.

There are significant differences in these rights and their political effects. While civil rights are a form of power, social rights refer to individuals as consumers, not actors. Thus Macpherson notes that: '... civil rights are rights against the state whereas social rights are claims for benefits guaranteed by the state.'[8] Democratic citizenship may provide the ideological basis for a theory of social and political integration, but it cannot overcome the inequalities of class. This is very apparent in immigrant politics where the issue of the effective exercise of social rights is a recurrent theme.

The state may create formal equality through citizenship – making migrants full legal members of the national community – but it cannot create social equality. In practice inequality means '... the practical ability to exercise the rights or legal capacities which constitute the status of citizen will not be available to all who possess them'.[9] The state may be able to create the legal basis of equality by guaranteeing rights but it cannot guarantee their actualisation.

The disadvantage of being an immigrant, of lacking full social rights – problems with convertible cultural capital such as lack of English language, recognised qualifications, education, social networks, social knowledge – has been addressed largely as an ethnic rather than class issue by the state. In this way, the social rights of citizenship have been converted into a problem of pluralism. From immigrants' own perspective, ethnicising claims is a way to speak for collectivities and to have ones' claims assessed as more deserving on the basis of ethnicity. Moreover, other kinds of collective rights are claimed such as law reform to recognise cultural (read ethnic) pluralism. Even political rights become ethnicised into collective constituencies as if votes were able to be delivered en bloc.

However, the struggle over the realisation of 'citizenship' rights is often an ambivalent one. In the tension between permanence and transience, immigrants are caught between negotiating the conditions of acceptance and retaining the cultural and social institutions which might allow return migration or the shift to another destination, the need to maintain access to parallel social worlds in other places.

Resistance to resocialisation as 'citizen' and proletarianisation on the one hand, and the positive valuation of culture and identity in a multicultural society on the other are two sides of the politics of cultural assertion. The cultural practice of immigrants is the medium of continuity and reinterpretation of tradition in radical ways which are transmitted to communities of origin and work new interpretations at home. Reinterpretations and feedback of immigrant culture to home communities are interactive. As Fischer observes of contemporary Iranian culture in America, '... [it is] woven on a geographically set loom, one beam set in Iran and one set abroad in America and Europe. Each end is itself a generative locus of *differance*, of identity, contributing new bits of warp and woof.'[10]

The interaction between immigrant and home cultures articulates a broader cultural and political relationship between North and South which is illuminated in migration through the immigrant experience of proletarianisation. That one's origin locates one in social space as an immigrant and generates a discourse about one's social trajectory expressed in terms of success and failure. The promise of greater control over one's life through migration to the North is increasingly being challenged by the uncertainties of fulfilment and acceptance leaving identity and cultural authenticity as the only vehicles to assert that control. Identity becomes a discourse constructed around different possibilities. Thus, for example, Islamic assertion and fundamentalist practice in migration can be a response to proletarianisation, social rejection and discrimination, as well as a product of the openness not found in communities of origin.[11]

Cities, Immigrants and Integration

The political economy of citizenship rights must be understood in the context of the site of immigrant incorporation. The realisation of rights occurs not so much in the 'nation state', the homogenising cultural space, as in the 'city', the pluralising and differentiating social space. Migrant settlement in the cities of the North has not just been a question of choice, a journey to modernity, but a measure of the importance of the city in capital accumulation. Cities are geographical entities which Harvey describes as having a 'structured coherence'. They act

> ... as a unity of job and consumption opportunities (shaping) ... the standards of living, the qualities and style of life, work satisfactions (or lack thereof), social hierarchies (authority structures in the workplace, status systems of consumption), and a whole set of sociological and psychological attitudes toward working, living, enjoying, entertaining, and the like.[12]

For migrants cities are the primary site of incorporation.

As the urban political economy has changed so too has the social trajectory of many migrants. In the immediate post-war years the industrial city was made the focus of capital investment organised around 'demand-side urbanisation' – suburbanisation.[13] Surplus labour and capital went into the development of built environments and the expansion of the social wage. 'Domestic-economy-building' focused on urban expansion, population growth and consumption rather than production. Migrant labour was a significant element in this model of development in the North. Large-scale immigration programmes, like that launched in Australia, were an integral part of suburbanisation strategies to ensure that labour needs were met.

Changes in the international division of labour brought changes in the pattern of capital accumulation and consequently in the political economy of cities. The emphasis shifted from the mobility of labour to the mobility of capital or 'flexible accumulation'. Under flexible accumulation cities were forced into competition for '... employment, investment, and new technologies ... by offering unique packages of physical and social infrastructures, qualities and quantities of labour power, input costs, lifestyles, tax systems, environmental qualities and the like.'[14] Investment, employment and urban expansion now depended on the capacity of cities to successfully promote themselves as specialised centres of production, consumption or finance.

Changes in the stability of the urban political economy altered the basis of participation and social integration of migrants. As the state adopted policies which favour capital over labour, the economic basis for migrants' opportunity and economic security has been undermined. Because wage costs figured prominently in the calculus of urban competition, migrants were the part of the population which became the most vulnerable to economic marginalisation through declining real incomes and unemployment. Technological displacement and/or deindustrialisation undermined job security and eroded the economic basis of generational social mobility.

In addition, state retreat from public spending intensified the experience of class inequality. Funds previously redistributed to broaden the consumption base and improve equality of opportunity across classes have been redirected to support investments in social and physical infrastructure 'to create favourable business environments'.[15] State policy supports the ' ... public subsidy of the consumption by the rich at the expense of local support of the social wage of the poor.'[16]

Changes in the political economy of the city have seen the very terms of migrants social and economic incorporation change. No longer can migrants assume generational cycles of incorporation and social mobility when the stability of cities are radically changing. Migrants face the problem of where they and their children will be incorporated, and on what terms. Their social trajectories will depend on their socialisation into specific labour arrangements and whether opportunities for unskilled workers continue to exist. Employment will also depend on their flexibility, willingness to accept work in the informal sector, or even the qualities of labour such as work attitudes and discipline. The common ethnic labour market classifications of 'good' and 'bad' workers are often summaries of a mix of perceived ethnic worker attributes. However, with increased instability in the patterns of class alliances, labour process and urban politics, migrants may well find themselves in structural positions precluding the possibility of social mobility.

The emergence of the global city, the city internationalised by new patterns of investment, but also by the internationalisation of work forces, has consequences for the social relations in which migrants' lives are embedded.[17] Firstly, the sustaining structures of immigrant family and community become the locus of the reproduction of labour, but also the locus of spheres of autonomy. This autonomy can be the basis of generational mobility or the reverse, the socialisation of migrants into restricted urban spaces, ghettos where life experience is homogenised and generationally transmitted. These 'small cultures' – cultures selectively recreated in migration by communities – are locally created comprehending the importance of place and community in global transformation.

Secondly, race, gender, religion and ethnicity are increasingly used as a means of control for '… selective integration of new labour supplies into an existing labour market'.[18] Under 'flexible accumulation' the state withdraws from areas of regulation as part of the process of informalisation. As a result there emerges a 'tolerated unregulated urban space' bringing the city in advanced capitalist countries closer to the Third World urban experience. In this context the politics of multiculturalism is an interstitial politics increasingly designed to regulate those not incorporated through normal processes.

Under these conditions the quality of migrant labour that will remain valued is their mobility which, in specific urban areas, will mean a temporary and/or marginal position sustained by the arrangements of the informal economy. These migrants are the object of what Offe refers to as negative labour market policies through which the state seeks to reduce the number of workers seeking jobs.[19]

Such policies include early retirement schemes, prohibitions on employing illegal immigrants, incentives for migrants to return home and subsidies for self-employment and small business.[20]

High unemployment amongst migrant workers is symptomatic of their marginalisation in excluded spaces. In brief, sites of permanent migration may well generate social arrangements which have been characteristic of temporary labour, just as the emergence of informal economic sectors in advanced industrial cities parallels development patterns in Third World cities.

Increased inter-urban competition will heighten the perception of sites of settlement as either uncertain or temporary. It will only sharpen the 'immigrant condition' of anticipated return and emphasise the significance of maintaining ties, and hence constantly weighing up alternative social trajectories in other sites – home communities or other communities in the diaspora. Politically, the impact of uncertainty about social mobility – or even maintaining current lifestyles – tends to emphasise local over broader class identities. The retention of cultural identity then becomes not merely resistance to incorporation but a strategy of retaining other choices which continue to exist in other possible destinations.

Multiculturalism

In Australia the high degree of cultural pluralism generated by immigration policies, and brought together in the principal industrial cities, has seen the state respond by adopting a pluralist definition of the 'nation'. The national policy of multiculturalism is both a description of society and new way to blur the manifestations of disadvantage as cultural. In a context where the state has been withdrawing from its earlier commitment to maintain the 'social wage', it has provided a mechanism to differentiate opportunity and access to redistributive policy from the state. Multiculturalism is a conservative strategy which enables the state to represent itself as maintaining a concern about the social wage – especially of poor immigrants – through redistributive policies, yet in the context of diminishing levels of finances allocated. The personalisation of ties through patronage facilitates the illusion of the maintenance of social benefits through the redistributive struggle of ethnic groups, producing thereby a way to direct competition within the culturally diverse working class.

When 'demand-side-urbanisation' permitted the continual replacement of unskilled labour through sustained migration, the idea that social mobility was the product of individual and even group effort could have currency. But the changing social and political contours of the city make such beliefs much harder to sustain. After all, if success is due in this equation to effort and desirable ethnic attributes, then failure is the product of the reverse.

The concept 'urban process' emphasises the interactive dimension of 'community formation' amongst immigrants; that cultural relations are simultaneously shaped by and are the product of the social spaces they inhabit. As urban class alliances, labour process and politics become more shifting then the system of symbolic consumption and social hierarchies also changes and becomes less certain. Community and ethnic identity may draw from cultural and social continuities, but they achieve their specific expression in the environment in which they are recreated. In other words, the cultural knowledge, organisation and identity immigrants bring with them are engaged in changing urban settings whose political economy is itself fluid. The analysis of immigrant communities and their incorporation must not 'force' the continuity of shared culture and social ties with earlier generations of Lebanese immigrants in understanding their likely destinies in the host society.

This forcing of tradition is part of the problem of homogenisation. Multiculturalism is derivative of the nation project, of the project of social standardisation. Multiculturalism is a phenomenon which is contingent upon the nation state and its strategy of social incorporation. As Spivak comments, homogenisation is controlling '... the whole notion of authenticity, of the authentic migrant experience, is one that comes to us constructed by hegemonic voices.'[21] The very construction of ethnicity is treated as unproblematic, accepting the Other as an authentic voice speaking for others like the traditional native informant with objective knowledge.[22]

Past, Present and Future

The changing political economy of cities endows migrants' connections with their past lives with practical as well as sentimental significance. Migrants continue to have a foot in two worlds – the present and the past – because the preservation of the past has increasingly become the basis for the formation of international cultures located in the growing uncertainties of individual lives and national histories.

Studies of immigrant communities must comprehend the ambiguity in social life generated through international migration and the urban process which now dominates the international mobilisation of labour. Dislocation and relocation produce a tension between permanence and transience which is articulated in a cultural dialogue which interacts with the past and the possibilities of the future conceived geographically and socially.

Counterpoised to the process of national incorporation is the persistent belief in the possibilities of return, the choice to resume past lives migrants commonly feel they have merely suspended, left in limbo, and which remain available for reactivation. The highly personalised character of the immigrant cultural world regenerated in settlement is thus often ambivalent about the future. Immigrant culture becomes a dimension of working class culture, but also constitutes a resistance to class location and the demand to submit to its cultural and social dictates. Thus immigrant culture contains within it both the seeds of incorporation and resistance, retaining the hope of return to social trajectories and lives abandoned – ironically with economic and cultural capital accrued through migration.

The cultural dialogue which engages the past and the future is articulated between a local and global arena. Migrants regenerate cultures, identities and communities locally; but they are also drawn into international discourse on cultural identities and political relations between North and South. What links the local and the global is a cultural elaboration or history explaining the predicament and future of a particular group. Local identities forged in the city are interconnected to a variety of supra-local discourses on cultural identity and social membership. These can have fairly limited dimensions such as family or village community within a global context as well as broader 'imagined communities' such as diaspora, national and transnational identities and histories.

The Muslim immigrant communities which are the focus of this study articulate their local social practice and cultural identities within the broader context of family reciprocities, community ties, debates about national identity and Islamic assertions. The migrant experience becomes intertwined with transnational cultural movements which have emerged in the context of the crisis of the post-colonial nation state. The remaking of Islam in the West has two axes, the localisation of community and identity in the industrial city, and the resistance to the 'cultural imperialism' of the West. The latter is expressed through the strategies of the conservation of orthodox religious practice and the defence of patriarchal values in the family in the West. Concern in Islamic centres in the Muslim world over the loss of faith amongst immigrants and their separation from the *'umma* has stimulated intervention to preserve their faith. Finance is provided to build mosques, found Muslim schools, import imams to provide religious guidance and education and even intervene politically in Muslim immigrant populations to alert them to the precarious character of their faith in the West. The pronouncement of the *fatwa* against Salman Rushdie was a warning for all Muslims about the 'corrupting' influence of Western society and the threat of apostasy.

Modern memory, as Paul Fussell argues, draws on past events which are seen as defining of cultural truth.[23] In Western European culture the Great War has been transformed '... into a "subject" and simplifies its motifs into myths and figures expressive of the modern existential predicament.' The images of violence of the war called 'Great' invade the mind and are employed to explore the identity of victimhood of the present. For the Islamic world, the experience and encounter with Western imperialism is the touchstone for interpretation of twentieth-century experience whether that be Arab nationalism, the establishment of Israel, decolonisation, the crisis of secular nation states or contemporary civil wars. Muslim Lebanese immigrants are culturally enmeshed in their own story of Muslim decline, nationhood and imperialist intervention in Lebanon. It is the resonances of this story that Muslim immigrants draw upon in their understanding of their personal and communal lives. Moreover, even if individuals formulate their sense of self independently of their pasts, they are constantly reminded by the dominant culture that their difference connects them to cultural and political struggles in the Muslim world. The surge of anti-Muslim and Arab feeling during the Gulf War led many Australian Muslims to point out that they should not be blamed for events in the Middle East – but they were!

This reservoir of narratives about the self and community has opened up at a time when the locus of belonging is no longer easily geographically bounded by national societies. Reference to the past and tradition by immigrants is being challenged by social dispersal and local encounters of Others – the identity generated by multiculturalism. At a time when Islamic fundamentalist movements seek to strictly limit the possibility of interpreting the 'Word', migrants are forced to engage a complex world through more open interpretation of tradition. From the Muslim world the threat of contagion – the loss of believers and the reimporting of new interpretations of tradition into the Muslim heartland – was expressed in the passionate and militant reaction towards Salman Rushdie. It was a fundamental challenge to a 'readerly' narrative of origins and history in which self-realisation could only be fulfilled through the story. The Western frontiers actually represented an opening which might engender scepticism about the authority of tradition; the possibility of challenging the Word through the engagement of traditions in new spaces constructed by relations outside their control.

2

The Refugees

> Our parents, having come to a place where their qualifications in medicine and law were unacceptable, had been forced to take work as labourers or factory hands or to keep dingy shops; but we, their clever sons and daughters would find our way back to the safe professional classes. (David Malouf *Southern Skies*, in Antipodes, Penguin: Ringwood Victoria, 1985)

The social world can be represented as 'social space' in which 'agents and groups of agents are thus defined by their relative positions within that space'.[1] Yet social space is not a given but a social product which is experienced, translated and transformed.[2] Immigrants' location in social space involves a recreation of social arrangements and a positioning of them in an unfamiliar world. The capacity to act in this new social space is shaped by the capital, both cultural and material, individuals possess.[3] They have to recreate and re-learn their 'habitus', their familiar social world, and acquire new capital if they wish to improve their social positions.

The world migrants create in the city is not determined by their agency, by their ability to carve out a sphere of autonomy through creating their 'habitus' according to the blueprints of tradition. Spatiality is an implicit, but secondary, aspect of the idea of 'habitus' whose main focus is cultural production. The social space that immigrants enter is urbanised space which is the locus of the reproduction of capitalist relations and a focus of state regulation. It is a fragmented, homogenised and hierarchically structured space.[4] Immigrants' habitus is the outcome of their encounter with urban space which has been, in one sense, created for them as labour, and necessarily occupied by them. Their migration and urban experience is not simply a question of exercising choice, 'one's right to opt out of the continuum of history, choosing isolation over community, and one's desires over one's obligations.'[5]

The act of migration sees old advantages – statuses, savings, networks – either lost or devalued in a double sense. Firstly, because transposed cultural capital is differentially valued in immigrant communities and the wider society and, secondly, because the very act of migration puts immigrants in the position of devaluing their own background, and being devalued by virtue of leaving their country of origin.

Recent changes in the urban process, the shift to 'flexible accumulation', have made urban space increasingly unstable. For migrants this means that permanent settlement has become increasingly uncertain as the very durability of the urban context is undermined. Immigrants can no longer presume to construct their social trajectory by reference to earlier immigrant experience of inter-generational mobility. No longer can the path of slow acquisition of desirable cultural capital be considered secure.[6]

The relationship between location and cultural practice amongst immigrants in Australia is primarily a question about the nature of social organisation in the contemporary industrial city. The market imperative in the movement of labour from South to North, as Mingione argues, takes place '… within historically established conditions of social organisation, shaped by complex mixes of reciprocity and redistribution.'[7] It is in the relationship between redistributive and reciprocal systems of socialisation that the issue of cultural practice must be explored. Tradition – Islamic culture and practice – is re-formed through international migration and provides a medium through which the new world is apprehended and managed. The process of apprehension and proletarianisation takes place through the medium of the old:

> Having arrived at an urban centre, the migrant starts to experience a complex of pressures: class exploitation, transforming him into a proletarian; multiple pressures of urban society – problems of housing, health, education, through which he enters into a dialectical and conflictual relationship with the state ... Under these circumstances, a natural reaction would be to assert the symbols and ideological values of the society from which he has come, in order to express his antagonism towards the new society which exploits him.. Superficially this would seem to be the survival of the old elements, but in reality, behind this survival is concealed a transformation: these 'rural elements' are simply the raw materials in order to express new antagonisms ...[8]

Lebanese Muslim immigrants have entered Australian society through the cultural mediums of family, community and religion which have located them in social space shaping their status, employment and residence patterns in Sydney. This process of social location involves, on the one hand, changes in the meaning of cultural practices and, on the other hand, the workings of cultural logic in a new social context. Cultural practices must be understood as part of a political economy of agency worked out within specific historical and institutional settings. Hence the creation of community life and Islamic practices amongst Lebanese Muslim immigrants in Australia is the historical product initially of the process of state formation and national incorporation in Lebanon, and subsequently through labour migration and national incorporation in Australia. Islam in this case, is recreated in a Western frontier, delimited by its structures of interpretation and authority.

This chapter charts the historical contingencies of Lebanese Muslim cultural practice in Australia and the ways it has been shaped by the broader themes of proletarianisation, the urban process and the formation of nation states. The next considers the same themes in Lebanon. An important point of comparison is the very concept of community and its role in social integration, particularly in nation states whose official ideology espouses cultural pluralism. Lebanese pluralism assumes the inequality of collectivities while the Australian case assumes their equality.

Cultural identity, however, is closely connected to the interplay between the associative and reciprocal patterns of socialisation. The cultural value of tradition is in flux because the very basis of incorporation is becoming fragmented. The capacity of the Fordist-welfare state to intervene to regulate the inequities of the labour market, and to compensate for inadequacies of wage incomes through welfare provisions is diminished. This has made urban subsistence focused on social reciprocities increasingly important for immigrants.

The cultural world of immigrants is thus localised within allocated urban space and connected internationally through the versatilities of reciprocity which can connect different spaces. The duality of particularism and internationalisation of identities is part of life in the contemporary industrial city. 'The logic of globalisation has brought together diverse cultures, in new and multiple combinations, within urban spaces.'[9]

The Setting

The post-civil war (1975) Lebanese immigrants, the focus of this study, were a fragment of the population exodus brought about by the destruction of Lebanon. These 'refugees', a status they were never officially accorded in Australia, were in many cases connected with established Lebanese immigrant communities, sections of which had migrated to Australia over 100 years earlier.

These Lebanese families and communities were the essential social and political conduit for the refugees' recruitment and settlement in Australia. Had the Australian Lebanese communities not existed there would have been no connection with Australian society, and therefore no ethnic voice to claim them as people in need of special consideration and care by the Australian government and public opinion. Hence the ties of family, community and religion formed the basis of cultural capital used to mobilise connections internationally and make political demands on the Australian state and to relocate people in social space.

The importance of social reciprocity as the basis of immigrant settlement was emphasised at the outset by the failure of the post-war Lebanese to gain official recognition as refugees. The Lebanese had in fact always been self-recruiting and supporting unlike many other immigrant groups who received government assistance to immigrate to Australia. The only period they received any significant assistance was between 1973–75 when 2,439 Lebanese, or half those coming to Australia in that period, were given assisted passages. Hardly any of those who arrived in 1976–78, in flight from the Civil War, received any assistance. In official parlance they were 'quasi-refugees' who were treated as normal immigrants.[10]

The state extended its established practice of relying on family and community self-help to facilitate settlement by permitting relatives to sponsor family under special 'humanitarian conditions'. They relied on private self-help rather than direct government welfare support for their settlement.[11] While refugees were immediately entitled to state health and unemployment benefits, primary responsibility for providing airfares, housing, employment and local knowledge fell heavily upon resident family and community members.[12]

The social relocation and incorporation of the refugees in Australian society was strongly shaped by their relationship to the established Lebanese communities. These communities were mainly from Maronite, Orthodox and Sunni communities from north Lebanon. The oldest were from villages around Becharri – the centenary of Lebanese presence in Australia was celebrated in 1980 by the Kfar Sgharb Association, a village close to Becharri – and from Tripoli and its environs, especially the Khoura and some from Akkar.[13] The later migrants came from different parts of the country, but often via Beirut where they had initially been involved in rural-urban migration. Most Shi'i migrants had followed this route to Sydney.

Because most refugees were from the rural and urban poor of Lebanon few had the cultural capital (especially qualifications and English language) to secure skilled or professional work. In this situation their Lebanese social connections were an important resource to provide for basic needs within a culturally diverse immigrant working class. However the social and cultural capital the refugees brought from their 'other lives' connected them differentially with the existing Lebanese immigrant communities and organisations.[14] In general the social connections and institutional support of those from Maronite and Orthodox sects had greater generational depth than those from Muslim Sunni or Shi'i background. This was the historical outcome of earlier patterns of Lebanese immigration in which Lebanese Christians had predominated.

Entry into Australian society through existing Lebanese communities was a source of social and cultural comfort; but it also structurally located and culturally defined the refugees in the urban system. The social trajectory of the Lebanese refugees was shaped by the meaning of 'being Lebanese' in Australia – where they were located in the urban spatial hierarchy.

Lebanese Immigration

The social significance of 'being Lebanese' changed over the history of Lebanese migration to Australia. The Lebanese were a non-

English speaking (NES) immigrant group who, like all NES immigrants, faced discrimination from a dominant white settler society.[15] At first Lebanese migrants were a small and largely unnoticed group who generally fitted into Australian society on the margins of commerce. The image of the early Lebanese immigrant as hawker and pedlar is a common one amongst many Lebanese immigrant communities throughout the Americas, the Carribean and West Africa from the l880s until the early 1930s.[16] The recent Lebanese refugees, by contrast, were a large conspicuous group many of whom found themselves in marginal employment or long-term unemployment.

Lebanese immigration to Australia can be periodised to highlight the changing position of the Lebanese in the context of Australian immigration.

i. The pre-1947 phase: characterised by individual and chain migration, small in scale and almost exclusively Christian Maronite and Orthodox dating back to 1881.
ii. The 1947–1966 phase: characterised by a significant increase in the number of immigrants, predominantly northern Lebanese Christians, but still relatively small in proportion to overall non-European immigration of this period of mass migration to Australia.
iii. The 1967–1975 phase: this saw a 200 per cent increase in the Lebanese immigrant population. This period coincided with the Australian government's drive for new sources of immigrants and a general increase in tension in the Middle East after the 1967 Arab–Israeli war.
iv. The post-1975 phase: was characterised by refugee migration from the Lebanese civil war when many Lebanese were granted special consideration to immigrate or extend their temporary stay in Australia. It was during this period that the sectarian origin of immigrants changed markedly to include around as many Christians as Muslims.

Before the period of mass immigration to Australia which began in 1947 there were only 1,886 Lebanese/Syrians resident in the country.[17] These early immigrants were part of the exodus of mainly Christian population which had resulted from the Ottoman decision to permit the emigration of subjects from the empire.[18] From 1860–1900 it is estimated that some 120,000 people had left Syria, the overwhelming majority from Lebanon.[19] Their main destinations were the United States, South America, West Africa, Canada, and Australia. Emigration peaked in the years 1900–14 when between 4,000 and 5,000 were leaving annually, denuding Mount Lebanon of over 100,000 people or a quarter of its population.[20] A further 90,000 left from 1921–1938, 10,000 of them going to French and British African colonies.[21]

During the early period the Lebanese confronted a strongly exclusionist 'White Australia' immigration policy which dated from Federation in 1901 – the change from colony to constitutional monarchy. Racism towards Lebanese/Syrians saw them engage in public debate over whether they were European or Asian. The chose to assimilate, arguing that they too were European and not Asian, by which they meant civilised. Their success in this enterprise was reflected in the careers of their grandchildren as prominent Australian businessmen, sportsmen, intellectuals and politicians.[22]

Table 2.1 shows that the 1947–64 phase continued the earlier pattern of Christian immigration – around 7,000 Lebanese from the predominantly Greek Orthodox and Maronite Catholic villages in north Lebanon representing an annual average intake of 389. Over the next 10 years (1965–75), the numbers of Lebanese immigrants accepted in Australia increased considerably, averaging 2,139 per year.[23] The immigrants remained predominantly Christian; but Sunni Muslims, mostly from around Tripoli, also began to arrive. In this period the number of Lebanese Muslim immigrants grew from around 1,000 to 7,960.[24]

The increased number of Lebanese was not so much an

expression of greater Lebanese interest in Australia as the result of geographical and cultural broadening of the Australian government's immigration programme. Shortfalls in annual immigration quotas caused by diminishing interest from the United Kingdom (the 'preferred' migrant source), and an increased number of return migrants, led the government to broaden its recruitment area to include Southern Europe and the Eastern Mediterranean. These Mediterranean migrants were recruited for 'dirty work', unskilled labour. But even with an increase in their numbers the Lebanese immigrants were not particularly conspicuous in the stream of much larger numbers of Italians, Yugoslavs and Greeks.[26]

Table 2.1: Lebanese–Born Population in Australia 1901–1989

Year	Lebanese Born	Year	Lebanese Born
1901	1,500	1966	10,568
1911	1,527	1971	24,214
1921	1,803	1976	33,424
1933	2,020	1978	50,723
1947	1,886	1981	49,617*
1954	3,861	1986	56,337
1961	7,253	1989	65,857**

Source: Derived from Census and Immigration statistics.[25]
* The decrease between 1978 and 1981 indicates return migration after the fighting had subsided.
** Until April 1989

Between 1976–78 the Australian government accepted just over 20,000 Lebanese under relaxed immigration criteria. However, not all remained. Several thousand returned to Lebanon leaving the total intake for the period 1976–81 at around 17,000. During the 5-year period (1976–81) the Lebanese intake rose to an average of 3,400 per year representing a 44 per cent increase on the earlier 10-year period (1965–75).

In the post-1975 period the pattern of immigration was very irregular. Lebanese visiting on tourist visas were often permitted to extend their stay for prolonged periods by Australian immigration authorities due to outbreaks of fighting in Lebanon. The Department of Immigration and Ethnic Affairs also showed flexibility towards requests to convert temporary rights of residence into permanent residence. However, after the initial surge of refugees between 1976–78, immigration from Lebanon was carefully controlled. The combined effect of restricting visas and the relocation of the Australian Embassy in Lebanon to Damascus was to limit the number of Lebanese entering Australia. The cutback on accepting Lebanese immigrants saw on average only 1,261 per year arrive between 1978–90.

The surge of Lebanese refugees amounted to an accelerated 'chain migration' into the existing communities. Sponsorship of family and friends had been the most common pattern of migration amongst many Mediterranean migrants. However, the process of recruitment and settlement, which normally took place over one or two decades, was telescoped into six months. This accelerated chain migration was sanctioned by the Department of Immigration's strategy of approving lists of families drawn up by community representatives in Sydney. The consequence of adopting an even-handed policy for all sectarian communities was to reinforce sect as the key factor in all subsequent dealings with Lebanese immigrant organisations.

This social compression of Lebanese migration dramatically changed the size, concentration and composition of the Lebanese communities in Australia. It increased by more than half the number of Lebanese-born in Australia to around 52,000, further concentrated Lebanese settlement in Sydney and significantly changed the sectarian composition of the Lebanese communities by introducing a much larger number of Muslim migrants. In this period the Lebanese became known as a 'problem' community because of the sectarian tensions they had brought from the civil war and because of their poverty and unemployment in a protracted period of economic recession.

Migration and the Urban Process

Immigrants to Australia have been overwhelmingly concentrated in the cities and have represented a key element in their growth, especially the cities of Sydney and Melbourne where around 40 per cent of the national population live. In the post-1947 period 'demand-side urbanisation' (suburbanisation) made these cities the focus of investment in built environments. Immigrants served the dual role of providing labour for construction and manufacturing and increasing consumption in the domestic economy.

Unskilled labour was drawn disproportionately from non English-speaking migrants, two thirds of whom were concentrated in these two cities. The Lebanese settlement in these cities was even higher with 73 per cent of all Lebanese born immigrants in Australia concentrated in Sydney and 20 per cent in Melbourne.[27] Chain migration based on family and community ties strongly shaped their patterns of residential clustering. Personal connections located them in households, the labour and housing markets, and also in village-focused communities within distinct residential areas.

Family

But what was the character of family and community which provided the conduit of urban settlement? To say they were Lebanese only informs us of the personal basis of connections, elements of cultural memory and practices. The kind of families many Lebanese immigrants came from were productive households where family members were integrated into economic activities of farming, small crafts or commerce. To attribute cultural models emphasising patrilineality, cousin marriage and patriarchy is not in itself particularly informative without knowing their contexts.

A distinctive feature of South–North migration is the shift of households from forms of subsistence, or partial subsistence, to a much greater reliance on monetary incomes. The very recruitment of labour is premised on the assumption that people are willing to become wage workers, to be proletarianised. Industrial capitalism generated urban space to make people available as surplus labour. The constant evaluation of the worth of migrants as desirable or undesirable is invariably sheeted home to the question of their willingness to become productive wage workers.

Historically the process of drawing people into wage labour has been complex and certainly not unilineal. In Europe the peasant-worker survived a long time, facilitating social reproduction of the household through a combination of subsistence and wage incomes. In colonial systems indigenous forms of subsistence (autonomy) often had to be destroyed in order to make people labourers.

Migration to Australia has made similar demands for proletarianisation. Yet the premise of immigration policy, especially with respect to Mediterranean immigrants, has been a reliance on reciprocity for their social integration. The state relied upon forms of self-support while insisting that migrants eventually assimilate. In other words, settlement was constructed around a combination of wage incomes and social reciprocity. The apparent 'naturalness' and continuity of cultural practices in migration must be understood as a response to new combinations of urban subsistence and monetary incomes.

Amongst the Lebanese, recruitment of members through chain migration has historically been the principle form of soliciting migration. But chain migration did not only express the resiliance of kinship in migration – the continuance of obligation to kin members despite geographical separation. State immigration policy shaped chain migration by creating the category of 'family reunion' which permitted sponsorship of a restricted range of kin. The state, therefore, played an integral part in shaping the character of obligations towards family members 'back home'. Obligations towards those who fell outside the state's definition of 'family' members could be supported directly through remittances or indirectly by using arranged marriages between cousins to facilitate migration.

Among the Lebanese the recruitment of kin members under the 'family reunion' or 'spouse and fiance' categories accounts for around 70 per cent of all immigrants.[28] The figures are similar amongst other Mediterranean immigrant groups – e.g. Greeks, (former) Yugoslavs and Italians. The 'family reunion' category is such an electorally sensitive issue that any cutback in migration intakes target the 'skilled' and 'business' categories first.

Arranged marriage is another important means of recruitment between households in Australia and Lebanon. Immigration statistics reveal that an equal number of men and women contract such marriages with partners in Lebanon.[29] Among these are a large number of parallel and cross-cousin marriages, much larger than was the usual practice amongst Muslim and Christian families in Lebanon.[30] The culturally 'preferred' form of marriage has thus been enhanced through migration, at least first generation migration, since it allows the fulfilment of kin obligations by securing residency rights and is believed to invest greater security in the marriage than the romance market!

The family character of Lebanese immigration has been apparent in its consistently high gender ratios since the turn of the century. Unlike the usual pattern of Mediterranean migrations (especially Italian and Greek) where single male workers migrated only later to sponsor wives, the great majority of Lebanese migrated as family units. Only in the last two decades did Greek and Italian immigrants achieve similar sex ratios to the Lebanese.[31]

The family character of emigration from Lebanon must be sought in the character of family and households in Lebanese society. Themes such as the persistence of productive households and placed-based societies, minority repression and the disenfranchisement of exile, rural underdevelopment and return migration are all relevant and will be taken up in the following chapter in the discussion on Lebanese state and society. However, the impact of family chain migration to Australia was to create particular kinds of social interdependencies on the one hand and a degree of self-sufficiency on the other.

Discussion of the 'Lebanese immigrant family' in the city must be understood in the context of the structuring patterns of socialisation. For the 'refugees' the depth of kinship connections was important in shaping the strategies and dependencies of settlement. But equally important was the capacity of the labour market to absorb new unskilled labour and the limited scope of government welfare support. Economic marginalisation and informalisation of work reinforced social dependencies. Urban space may have transformed social relationships, but not in the unilineal way often suggested by industrialisation. The meaning of kinship ties changed and so too did the community context in which they were set.[32]

The content of Lebanese immigrant family reciprocities cannot be deduced from a cultural model, or even from official ethnic versions of 'family life'. Integration into labour markets and households shapes the internal division of labour which can produce very divergent households and equally divergent reciprocities ranging from patriarchal to matriarchal.[33] In the former, strong hierarchical relations may emerge subjugating the young, and especially the women, to the interests and command of the head of household. The latter can emerge where men are absent for reasons of work, divorce or death. In this case women assume the responsibilities of mothering and decision-making about work, schooling, careers and family investments.

The character of households that emerge can be strongly influenced by the vicissitudes of life. Matriarchal structures can emerge from the liberating possibilities – misfortunes perhaps – of migration. Widowhood and divorce are two examples.

Making Matriarchies

A Maronite mother of five young sons was forced to assume responsibility for the whole family when her husband died only three days after arriving in Australia. She laboured in a factory and gradually acquired property to establish herself as a landlady. She married again for respectability in the community – the suspicion and social fear engendered by women living without a man dies hard – but always remained the head of the household. She supported her sons' education and made gifts of property to them when they married. The close ties between mother and sons continued to be expressed in a weekly dinner the sons shared with her alone, even those who had married with their own families (the single ones often took her along with them on holidays to give her a treat, even once on a cruise ship where they were out to have a good time!)

A Muslim example is that of a woman who found the migration experience liberating and divorced her husband to raise her family as a single parent, something that would have been almost impossible in Lebanon. She was attracted to the non-sectarian stance of the Syrian Socialist Nationalist Party and became an active member, as did her children when they grew up. She imparted her independence to her children, especially her daughter, who was encouraged to study to be a medical doctor. She graduated as a doctor and worked in a Lebanese area becoming an important reference point for many Lebanese Muslim and Christian women.

The actual composition of individual households is but a superficial indicator of reciprocities that exist or can be potentially reactivated at some later date. Reciprocities can persist between households which are geographically removed and apparently geographically isolated as nuclear households. The flexibility of households in space and time has led to them being described as 'potential households' – that group among which obligations persist despite their dispersal through migration and which members regard as having the potential to reassemble as a single household at some future time.[34] Thus it is regarded as a moral rather than physical entity in which boundaries between nuclear and extended households are unclear. In the case of Lebanese immigrant households the member ship of potential households can include kin who have remained in Lebanon as well as members who have migrated to different international destinations.

Domestic and migration cycles also shape the composition and character of household obligations. A common pattern in the migration cycle was that individuals lived in larger and more composite households on arrival in Australia which gradually, over time, became more nuclear and smaller. Thus one study found the average household of Lebanese immigrants on arrival in Sydney had 5.3 persons and consisted of only one-third nuclear households. These were essentially transitory arrangements, usually breaking up when members became more economically independent through employment or social welfare benefits. As they became more established, the average household size increased to 5.6 persons of which three-quarters were nuclear. By contrast, the average household immigrants left in Lebanon was much larger at 6.9 persons and much less nuclear (68 per cent).[35]

The establishment of nuclear households in migration often conceals different patterns of obligation between households. Khuri points out that the establishment of nuclear households amongst rural-urban migrants in Beirut in the early 1970s often coincided with the financial support of extended kin networks in the village.[36] Similar patterns were evident in Sydney Lebanese households. One Sunni Muslim family (two brothers in living in separate households) in Sydney was able to afford full-time care (a Sri Lankan domestic contract worker) for their ageing parents in Tripoli, something they would have found financially prohibitive in Australia. Services could be bought cheaply on the international labour market in order to fulfil obligations towards ageing parents in Lebanon from wages earned in Sydney. It was also common for parents to put their young children in the care of their grandparents in Lebanon in order to maximise the incomes of both spouses working in Sydney. Amongst Maronite Catholics children were occasionally sent to convents in Lebanon to be cared for by nuns.

Obligations between households emphasise the continuity of place-based consciousness – the village – amongst the Lebanese in migration. Family is still attached to community of origin defining, to varying degrees, one's identity and status in the circles of the immigrant communities.

Community

The idea of immigrant community implies solidarities built upon persisting ties from pre-migration lives. It has the nostalgic ring of the demise of gemeinschaft, something potentially lost in migration, something the city would destroy. However, community in migration is constructed out of the intersection of the social preferences of migrants and social differentiation engendered through the urban process.

In Lebanese culture sociality and community are the product of bonds created from the intimacy of everyday life. Community is the socialisation of space as cultural world and social dependence. Place and biography naturalise social relations and create a social world of known others. They also locate people in relations of inheritance, marriage, friendship, status, power and dependence, and demarcate those who share the life of community. One's identity is constructed in relation to the significant others defined as community. Moreover, when strangers (that is individuals who do not immediately recognise themselves as belonging to the same community) meet, their first task is to determine their relative positions and status based on family name and community of origin.

But while it is represented as a socially autonomous product, community is also an expression of historical modes of integration in wider social orders. Community defines intimate social space but it is at the same time a relational concept. The boundaries between communities are culturally demarcated yet fluid. Mixed marriages, for example, may be easily accommodated at certain times but at times of social upheaval they may not. From the outside the 'community' is the locus of ordering, taxing and regulating. The Ottoman *millet* system made community, in the broader sense of sectarian community, the political focus of imperial order. From the inside the social world of the village community serves as a template for constructing relations with the wider world. The world is 'anthropologised', made known by constructing all relations as if they were personal and engendered moral obligations.

In the industrial city community is also shaped by the way people are integrated into urban space. Different classes are able to command space in different ways. In the industrial city it is characteristically the poor who directly and visibly occupy urban space. Basic needs are fulfilled through daily interactions based on a 'mix of mutual aid and mutual predation'.[37] In the context of the cultural pluralisation of the city through immigration the term 'community' is often used to refer to the conspicuous ethnic occupation of urban space organised around a shared culture and social solidarity that pre-existed migration. Hence 'ethnic community' implies dense residential occupation of space culturally demarcated by distinct architectural styles, shops, religious institutions and even schools.

However, ethnic urban domains originally delineated by dense settlement can persist as symbolic centres with quite different social characteristics long after the dispersal of first and second generation families to other suburbs. Such ethnic urban spaces are no longer sites of entrapment where protection in the family and dependence on community ties reproduces marginality. China Towns, Little Italies, and Little Lebanons have emerged as commercialised centres of consumption as well as symbols of the persistence, durability and the authenticity of ethnic community as well as cultural capital. These ethnicised domains – according to popular ethnic maps of the city – become integral to claims of 'community' representation in the city, and the space where ethnic worlds of status are measured with reference to one's community peers. They are also tangible cultural expressions of the worth, wealth and respectability of an ethnic community. Those who have grown distant from their origins across generations can identify with these spatially-defined residual cultural centres. These 'lapsed ethnics' can visit and consume 'their' cuisine in preserved ethnic spaces and, along with the wider middle classes, can indulge their cosmopolitan tastes within the city. Such is the popular Lebanese district of Surry Hills and Redfern, the oldest area of Lebanese settlement near the central business district of Sydney. While second and third generation Christian families still live in the area, and the oldest Maronite and Orthodox churches are found there, it is no longer the centre of the Lebanese population.

Although the creation of ethnic urban space through ghettoisation is conspicuous, it is the most restricted means of commanding space in industrial cities. As Harvey notes; 'Those who built a sense of community across space found themselves with a distinct advantage over those who mobilised the principle of community in place.'[38] Capitalism engendered different forms of community, the most notable of which has been the nation, the pre-eminent form of community in modernity. The nation represented both a superior form of control over space and broadened the definition of community. The nation was an expression of new forms of class command, new forms of regulation which transcended locality.

Community in the industrial city emerges out of the process of residential differentiation on the one hand, and the social preferences of individuals on the other. However, the dominance of forces outside the individual in shaping the urban environment makes the scope of autonomy of community limited. Rather, the very notion of community becomes integral to restrictions on choice which engender the 'homogenisation of life experience' which reproduces values and patterns of socialisation within the division of labour.[39] Cultural repertoires are invoked to create social capital in situations of marginality yet not all groups have the same opportunity to realise 'a sense of cultural continuity and autonomous presence'.[40]

Among the Lebanese refugees community was built upon the reciprocities of households, the impact of economic marginality, and the homogenising impact of official multiculturalism. People settled where they had family, knew members of village communities, or where they shared religious membership culturally defined by Lebanese sectarianism. Everyday needs could be readily met in this ethnic urban space without the knowledge of English or a familiarity with the larger city. While apparently the product of enduring reciprocities the migrants were inheriting the residential choices their sponsors had made from their own urban experience. It was a mediating space between ignorance and local knowledge about services, welfare and employment, which could be shared through personal, and culturally friendly, networks.

The social density of Lebanese community spaces was reinforced by the concentration of Lebanese settlement in Sydney; more than three quarters of all Lebanese born immigrants have settled there.[41] Within the city there is a close correspondence between residence and community of origin in the suburbs settled by the immigrant working class. Muslims from north Lebanon can be found concentrated in the working class western suburbs of Lakemba, Campsie and Punchbowl (Canterbury Local Government Area) amongst the larger and older Christian communities from north Lebanon. The Lebanese Shi'a, primarily from South Lebanon and Beirut, settled in the southern suburbs of Arncliffe and Rockdale and the Alawites concentrated in nearby Carlton. The Maronites and Orthodox, by contrast, were more dispersed but still remained residentially clustered. The oldest area of settlement was Redfern while the more recent arrivals were located in Canterbury and Parramatta, the new focus of Maronite social and cultural life in the city.

Mutual aid and welfare has been a focal point of Lebanese community organisation and social fragmentation. Voluntary associations have proliferated among the Lebanese, although the actual number of organisations has been in constant flux. The official number of associations of all types – village, religious, political, social and sporting – rose from 35 in 1975, 101 in 1980, 119 in 1985 to 66 in 1987.[42] If unregistered groups are included, estimates reach up to 250 organisations in the early 1980s. Migration flows, the politicisation of ethnic identities as a result of the Lebanese civil war, and the opportunities for ethnic representation created by multiculturalism, have all influenced the formation and disappearance of organisations.

By far the most common organisation has been the village association. Others include welfare, religious, sporting and social associations. Attachment to locality, 'the village', is the focal point of community life. As in Lebanon, locality and family name still serve to map reciprocities and status. Graphic displays of this attachment in the form of large, stretched, photographs of the 'village' in the entrance halls of Lebanese households are quite common in Sydney. The visual summary of community in these photographs clearly links place and identity in the city. The centrality of the village association in immigration parallels the centrality of village community/urban quarter in Lebanese society.

The idea of the global village is a reality for many Lebanese. Not only do many maintain links with their communities of origin but also with parts of the village in the diaspora which has been formed from over a century of emigration.[43] As one member of the village of Bishmizzine commented about the experience of emigration 'We have been afflicted with too many advantages, but the worst of them is migration.'[44] The village was connected to the world through the links of chain migration which frequently continued over generations. Moreover emigration did not often lead to the destruction of the village through depopulation. The social space of local 'community' has been preserved by remittances to family households, high levels of return migration in the first half of the century, marriage and visiting.[45] In the villages of north Lebanon, especially around the Koura and Becharri, the process of the internationalisation of 'local community' is very evident. Here neighbouring villages have discrete links with very different parts of the world, most commonly in North America, South America or Australia. Historically the village connected people to the world unmediated by the state or broader social institutions.

In migration the village community, organised formally or informally, has also been the main interface between state and immigrants. Community associations grew out of the basic needs of settlement and were reinforced by state policy of welfare intervention which served to ethnicise urban space. At the height of tensions during the Lebanese civil war ethnic identity became extremely parochial. 'Ethnic' workers supported by state welfare grants were recruited on the very narrow grounds of cultural familiarity – not only sect, but region and even village origin. It was argued by village associations that only one of their own could be culturally sensitive enough to understand the needs of the village members. While family located people in households, community linked them to a familiar world of immigrant village communities where reciprocity between associations produced a cycle of functions, celebrations and visits.

Village associations were the basic units of the more broadly based community organisations which included branches of Lebanese political parties, religious institutions and welfare bodies. The social space of village community thus became incorporated into a wider articulation of interest in ethnic politics, of religious identity, and allegiance and support for causes in the civil war. A constant round of functions conspicuously delineated cultural and political boundaries confirmed by the circulation of donations and reciprocal invitations.

Village organisations are the focus of the politics of representation. The attempt to speak for others is the basis of claims of representation at various levels of incorporation within the immigrant communities. The 'president' of a village organisation may speak for the village 'community' even though all people from a village may not be actual members of the association. As Bourdieu observes 'The spokesperson, in speaking of a group, on behalf of a group, surreptitiously posits the existence of the group in question, institutes the group, through the magical operation that is inherent in any act of naming.'[46]

At the level of the ethnic group the issue of Lebanese representation has been contentious. Any attempt by individuals to claim this role has been immediately rejected by other members of the 'community' as sectarian. If the Lebanese did not have a single voice in Lebanon, how could they have one in Australia? In multicultural Australia ethnic representation is a matter of claims which are based on self-identification, not official state certification.

In addition, the claims to representation can be quite instrumental and personally based growing out of reputation politics rather than shared social reciprocities and need. The formation of the Saida Association is a case in point.

Vicarious Prestige
The Saida Association was only established in 1993. For years the Sunni immigrants from Saida had felt no need to form themselves into an association. The catalyst for the founding of the association was the appointment of a son of Saida, Rafiq Hariri, to the post of prime minister in Lebanon. The elevation of Hariri provided the opportunity to claim affinity with prestige on the basis of place of origin. Men interested in accruing status in the social circuit of village functions made the effort to form the association and create a new office of association president. The Lebanese ambassador was invited to the inaugural celebration to mark the importance of the occasion.

The broader religious organisations were based on a similar structure of village representation. Religious organisation grew out of sociality based on descent and locality as well as the state's preference for dealing with institutionally recognisable bodies, especially bureaucratised ones. Thus in migration religion, as well as being a matter of personal faith and spiritual values, became the basis for generating communal structures and identity beyond the village and an institutional vehicle for liaison between the state and an immigrant working class.

The social and administrative committees of the churches and mosques drew upon village associations to mobilise and socialise their congregations. The Maronite Church, for example, established a church council composed of representatives from village organisations and the Sunni mosque's administrative committee has been dominated by representatives from village associations. Struggles over the appointment of imams to the mosque has also revolved around village association politics.[47]

The historical nexus between community and religion in migration is reflected in the age of the churches and mosques. One measure of the length of residence of communities is the age of their religious institutions. The original centres of Lebanese settlement were in the inner-city suburbs of Redfern and Waterloo which contain the oldest Maronite, Orthodox and Melkite churches which were built in 1890, 1914 and 1895 respectively. The building of new Orthodox and Maronite churches in the 1960s and 1970s and the monastery of St Charbel reflected the changing locus of Lebanese settlement in the city.

By contrast the oldest 'Lebanese' mosque, the Imam Ali mosque in the Sunni neighbourhood in the western suburb of Lakemba, was not built until 1976 when there was an influx of Lebanese Muslims during the civil war. Its designation as a 'Lebanese' mosque is resented by the broader Australian Islamic associations. But even this designation is in fact too broad. It is a north Lebanese, Tripoli-focused, Sunni Muslim institution whose politics have revolved around the village-based associations of that region. Its imam was active in the formation of the radical Islamic movement which came to power in Tripoli from 1983–86.[48]

A new 'Lebanese' Shi'ite mosque, known as al-Zahra, was completed in the southern suburb of Arncliffe even more recently, in 1983. Its construction also grew out of the co-operation of Lebanese Shi'ite village associations. Mosque politics focused on the village but became increasingly organised around identification with local branches of Amal and Hizbollah. In the Shi'ite case the emergence of the mosque displaced an influential regional association, the South Lebanese Association, which, while focused on sect and village, had been secular and leftist in its political orientation. The Shi'ite immigrants only began to strongly identify with political Islam in the early 1980s at the time when militant Islamic movements emerged in Lebanon.

Mosque building itself emerged as a node in religious consciousness formation in the suburbs, mainly because of neighbourhood opposition to their establishment. Religion, however, was a pole of organisation and identity that evolved slowly. Community meeting places only gradually assumed the function of mosques. This was the case for both the Sunni and Shi'ite mosques which were both built on sites which had evolved from the premises of community associations to centres of religious activity as the number of Muslims in the area grew.

Lebanese Sunnis from Tripoli and Shi'ites from border villages around Bintijbail and Tibneen had established their original centres in 1961 and 1976 respectively. The practice of establishing mosques by stages generated considerable hostility amongst older Anglo–Australian residents of these neighbourhoods. Suburban houses were bought by associations as meeting halls and gradually assumed the role of mosques without prior local government permission for their use as places of worship. Invariably this generated strong resentment towards Muslims in the suburbs and led to neighbourhood campaigns to stop the building of mosques. Complaints to local councils usually focused on noise, traffic and parking problems; but they were also fuelled by a dose of racism. One municipal council campaign to prevent a site being used for a mosque solicited every local council in New South Wales to contribute money to a 'fighting fund' to defend its decision in the Land and Environment Court.[49] In another case in Bankstown, a western Sydney suburb, a candidate in a local government election even campaigned for a 'Mosque-free Zone'.[50]

The character of Lebanese religious community in migration has emphasised locality before the 'imagined community' of confession. Religious community in migration has invariably grown from the spiritual needs of immigrant communities whose social lives have remained strongly locality oriented. The pattern of religious community and institutions growing out of locality and kinship has been the predominant pattern amongst Muslim immigrants in Australia and also Western Europe. Local mosque communities have generally organised themselves in Britain, France, Belgium and Germany before the branches of different Islamic sects and movements have established themselves.[51]

In Australia the formation of the religious culture of most Mediterranean immigrants has experienced the tensions between locality and confession as the basis of membership and led to conflicts with official religious organisations. Branches of small churches have arrived after the formation of communities and frequently come into conflict with rites autonomously nurtured by individual clerics recruited by village communities. One prominent Maronite woman in the Baan Association in Thornleigh (a northern Sydney suburb) pointed out that as immigrants they had always been self sufficient, looking after their family and village members, bringing them to Australia, providing them with lodgings, finding them work and teaching them English. In their case the local Catholic church had ministered to the community's religious needs and educated their children.[52] The arrival of a Maronite bishop in 1974 assuming responsibility for the religious needs of all Maronites was seen as quite provocative by these village–community centred groups.

Mosques have also experienced similar tensions over the appointment and retention of imams recruited by village-based mosque committees. The absence of a central religious body or head of the religion has meant that the network of clerics, forged through learning, has provided the basis of recruitment. In Sydney this has led to struggles to depose imams as different factions in mosque committees gain ascendancy and seek imams from different clerical networks.[53] I will return to these conflicts later in the discussion of the cultural politics of Islam in migration.

The social space of 'community' in migration is not, however, autonomously defined. Immigration creates a potential rearrangement of the currency of kinship and status. Khuri describes the role of political patronage in the formation of family associations among rural immigrants in Beirut within a new political environment.[54] In Sydney legal regulation of associations and eligibility of government welfare grants shape the structure of organisations. Hence the Charitable Associations Act regulates the formation of community associations and provides for the annual election of office holders. Village politics come to court when contested election results are appealed on the basis of legal rules of association and election. Informal associations do exist but they forfeit the potential economic and status benefits conferred by registration. These include eligibility to apply for government grants for welfare and cultural projects and the enhanced claims of representation that flow from official recognition as a recipient of a welfare grant.

State policy towards the integration of immigrants has also shaped community organisation and identity. At the time of arrival of the Lebanese refugees 'ethnic community' had already begun to assume a broader political significance in the context of the official policy of multiculturalism. 'Multiculturalism' mobilised demands on the basis of ethnic interest groups which were often 'paid' for by adjusting intakes in immigration categories – a perennially sensitive area among immigrants who were constantly trying to bring more family members to Australia. The acceptance of Lebanese refugee families dovetailed with government use of family reunion as a concession in redistributive ethnic politics and the use of kinship as a strategy for urban subsistence. During the early 1980s more than half of the arrivals came under the family reunion and refugee humanitarian categories.[55] This pattern of recruitment of family members and spouse in the context of multicultural politics mirrored similar trends in US immigration policy.[56] In other words, Lebanese sectarian demands for increased immigration coincided with the expansion of the politics of multiculturalism which became strongly focused on the issues of family and community settlement.

Communities had always played a role in the process of incorporation with mutual aid societies providing assistance, housing and local knowledge. Now, within the new politics of multiculturalism, they act as a medium of socialisation and representation separate from the workplace and labour organisations. In cities with large immigrant populations, voluntary organisations have assumed an important role in the assimilation of the unintegrated immigrant working class. They are focal points of recruitment, settlement, information, labour market entry, and regulation in the politics of ethnic representation generated under multiculturalism.

However, the sheer number of Lebanese associations presented considerable difficulties for government agencies in managing 'the Lebanese', especially in allocating funds for self-help welfare projects. 'The Lebanese Settlement Council', a body representing all official Lebanese associations, was created so that through it they could be managed. This subsequently became an elected body, 'The Lebanese Council', whose brief was to provide services for all – a very ambitious project given the state of sectarian relations in Lebanon at the time.

'Community' became an important focus in the articulation of difference in the post-refugee period. The ideological and political conflicts of the civil war were mobilised afresh forging distinctive Lebanese identities in ethnic politics. The proletarianisation of Lebanese immigrants in fact involved recreating kinship and sectarian loyalties to promote a social endogamy based on religious affiliation. For the earlier generations it reactivated connections with their Lebanese past. Fund-raising campaigns were organised for village communities they had long since lost touch with in order to give content to lapsed cultural and historical knowledge in the context of civil war.

Social identity became increasingly articulated in terms of sect as the incorporating identity. Religious institutions and religious practice provided the focus of organisation and the mobilisation of support through participation. Religion was strongly identified with community, reinforced by the politics of multiculturalism.

The cultural world of these immigrant communities was also informed by a vigorous Lebanese Arabic press which articulated many different political currents and identities. Newspapers were strongly identified with particular communities and the political fragments of the Lebanese war. The cultural world each paper embraced was graphically depicted in their social pages where photographs of weddings, functions and meetings delineated their 'community', while news reports summarised visions of Middle East and Lebanese politics from a sectarian perspective. The number of publications rose and fell with the variable intensity of the conflict in Lebanon and its translation into political rivalry in Sydney. To have one's own publication was claim to influence and status in the community arena, even if the circulation was small and the publication a financial liability.

Arabic newspapers, newsletters and radio programmes have been the principal cultural mediums of communication about the 'community' and provided daily news about Lebanon. The principal Arabic newspapers and weekly magazines are *An Nahar* (The Day), *Saout el Moghtareb* (Voice of the Migrant), *Al Watan* (The Motherland), and *al Bairak*. Smaller publications published on a monthly or bi-monthly basis include *Al-Daawah* (The Message), *Al Mouharer* (The Editor) and *El Wikalat* (The Agency). Various newsletters are circulated by village associations to inform members about social functions and religious calendar events. However, since the late 1970s numerous papers have disappeared including *An-Nahda* (The Renaissance), *Sada Lobnan* (The Echo of Lebanon), and *Al Akhbar* (The News) because of lack of finances or declining interest in political positions eclipsed by the course of the war.

In addition to the newspapers media and newsletters there are several Arabic radio programmes. The most important is the Arabic programme on 2EA, a government-supported ethnic radio station, which is broadcast daily for around an hour. A new ethnic station called 'Radio 2000' also broadcasts Arabic language programmes. 'Community access' radio, 2SER-FM, provides slots for groups to produce their own programmes. 'The Lebanese

Programme' and 'The Cedars of Lebanon Folkloric Group' each broadcast for an hour once a week.

Proletarianisation

The other important factor which shaped community was the experience of proletarianisation. While the conduit for entry into Australian society was households and communities, Lebanese access to employment was fundamentally determined by the labour market – the structure of work, conditions, pay and job security. For all migrants economic opportunity is primarily related not to ethnic identity but to the cultural capital (education, language, qualifications) necessary to compete in the Australian labour market. For most working class Lebanese the choice of employment was limited because of lack of skills, qualifications or English. This was also the case for skilled workers and professionals whose qualifications were devalued by non-recognition. Consequently they entered unskilled occupations where the English language requirement was minimal or they sought self-employment in a small business requiring low capital investment and often minimal English, especially if it was directed at Lebanese consumers. The most common Lebanese family business is the corner store, often referred to as a 'mixed business'.

The image of the Lebanese immigrant as small businessman dies hard. It may well have been the case that in Australia, as in the Americas, the early 'Lebanese' immigrant was typically a hawker or pedlar and then small shopkeeper.[57] The early Lebanese in New South Wales were heavily involved in commerce. However, this declined from a high of 94 per cent in 1901 to 35 per cent in 1947.[58] Accurate statistics on the occupational status of self-employment for Lebanese are unavailable for this period, but if the pattern of self-employment amongst other Mediterranean migrants (Greeks,

Italians, Yugoslavs) is taken as a guide then the levels of self-employment were probably between 20–30 per cent. While the image of 'businessman' or 'small trader' still survives, the reality is that almost 80 per cent of Lebanese were employees in 1981. Only 15 per cent were self-employed; this figure is, nevertheless, still 50 per cent higher than that for the Australian-born population among whom 10 per cent are self-employed.[59]

There are many family business success stories which serve to validate the ethnic legend of early Christian Maronite, Orthodox and Melkite Lebanese families to Australia. Some of the most prominent of these in Sydney include the Scarfs, Mansours, Gazals, Moubaraks, Abouds, and Maloufs in manufacturing and finance businesses; Shehadie, Alam and Katter in political and public life, and the Simons, Solomons, Becharas, and Whebbes in the development and construction industries. In many cases these businesses have become such a familiar part of the Sydney commercial landscape that Anglo–Australians are quite unaware of their Lebanese origins.

However, most Lebanese have shared the employment experience of the non-English speaking immigrant working class ending up in unskilled jobs, experiencing higher levels of unemployment and earning lower average weekly earnings than the Australian-born population. Even those with professional or skilled qualifications have found it extremely difficult to have them recognised in Australia. Professional bodies and trades have strictly regulated their entry into professional and skilled areas by insisting on Australian training. Migration is often deskilling, even for qualified professionals.

The main source of employment for non English-speaking migrants has been unskilled work. According to the 1981 census 56.4 per cent of Lebanese, 59.4 per cent of Italian and 73 per cent of Yugoslav migrants were employed in manufacturing and construction compared with only 37 per cent of Australian-born workers.[60] A very similar pattern was found in the Lebanese-born population in

Sydney. Almost half the employed males and 55 per cent of the employed females were in factory or labouring jobs.[61]

Since the early 1980s unemployment fell disproportionately on the non English-speaking immigrants who suffered three to four times the national average levels of unemployment. In the case of the two most recent large refugee groups, the Lebanese and Vietnamese, these levels have remained chronically high – up to 40 per cent – despite significant improvement in the national unemployment levels in the late 1980s.

The main factors affecting unemployment amongst Lebanese have been their low education levels, lack of English, participation in unskilled work and large households with young children.[62] In other words the employment opportunities for unskilled, poorly educated, non-English speaking men and women were not great at a time of recession and decline in the manufacturing industry.[63]

The impact of length of residence, educational and language differences, was very evident in the differential labour market positions of the different sectarian communities. Not only were there considerable differences between the Lebanese-born Christian and Muslim populations, but also between the Sunni and Shi'a populations. The Sunni men and women had the lowest employment participation rates: 43 per cent and 14 per cent respectively. This compared with the overall Lebanese sample in which 65 per cent of men and 28 per cent of women were in the employment. In marked contrast to the Sunni the Shi'i men (70 per cent) and Shi'i women (29 per cent) had much higher participation rates. By sect, the Sunni males had the highest concentration of employment in unskilled work at 75 per cent, much higher than the concentration of Shi'i (53 per cent), Antiochian (52 per cent) and Maronite (45 per cent) males.

The youthfulness and size of Muslim immigrant households contributed to the lower participation rates of Muslim women. Large households and a high proportion of children under five years of age placed heavy childcare and domestic work responsibilities on the women in these families. The Sunni had the largest average household size of 6.2 persons and the largest proportion of children under 5 years at 20 per cent. The Shi'a also had large households 5.6 and 14 per cent of under 5 years.

One marked difference between the Sunni and Shi'i households which influenced the participation of women in the labour market was the maintenance of a close-knit community strongly focused on village origin. The Shi'i households were more socially compact in origin – they came from a small number of border villages in South Lebanon – more concentrated in settlement than the Sunni, which meant they could draw on a range of kin and community ties more readily for childcare. Moreover, in the early 1970s, the Shi'a had also consciously organised households to maximise labour market participation. Prior to the war it had been quite common amongst Shi'i families to send young children home to their grandparents in Lebanon to allow both parents to work and maximise family income.

Among marginally employed groups such as Lebanese refugees, labour market participation rates are not particularly informative about the economic functioning of households. Participation rates measure employment of any kind – full-time, part-time or casual – and not the adequacy of incomes for living. To have a job does not necessarily markedly improve your position as a consumer, especially if a low wage is earned from a casual job. Such employment can actually cost more than it is worth because of the loss of entitlement to welfare benefits like free health care, travel concessions on public transport and subsidies services.

Many of these households in fact continued to function as productive households, even where members had separate wage incomes. The household was the focus of urban subsistence organised around social reciprocities of kinship and mixed monetary incomes.[64] In it all incomes were pooled and disbursed by the head of household.

The most cohesive economic household units were family businesses which exclusively employed their own members. In this case no money was disbursed as wages. However, the independence implied in these family small businesses was more illusory than real. The exploitative nature of family businesses suggests that marginal workers become marginal entrepreneurs.[65] Family businesses are labour intensive, based on small returns for long hours of work. They are also highly vulnerable to failure in Australia and the frequency with which small Lebanese businesses burn down suggests that they share this vulnerability.[66]

Another feature of these family businesses is their job creation role in marginal groups. Encouragement of small business is a way for governments to reduce official unemployment statistics – a preoccupation in the Western world. However, within these family businesses, and sometimes even in successful ones, individual members continue to behave as marginals by continuing to collect unemployment and exploiting subsidies. This amounts to continued state subsidy, albeit small, for the operation of marginal small businesses. The following story illustrates the way the socialisation of marginality can persist even amongst successful families.

Marginality and Family Business

Majid was a 23-year-old from a Sunni family from Tripoli. He had arrived in Australia at the age of three and had grown up in Sydney. His father ran a family business making clothes. It began as a small enterprise running from home with family labour and later expanded to become three factories located in Sydney and Brisbane, the capital city of the state of Queensland over 1,000 kilometers to the north. Majid was involved in the business from the age of 14 and was now a skilled production organiser and seller. However, despite the relative success of the family, Majid still behaved as if they were poor. For several years he received unemployment benefits while working for the business. To save money he even travelled by inter-state coach to other federal capitals, journeys which took 14 hours, rather than the one-hour plane trip. The coach fare was not only cheap, it allowed him to use the public transport concession pass to which he was entitled with his unemployment benefits. In fact he sometimes bought two seats at concessional rates so the long coach journey would be more comfortable.

Urban subsistence was more commonly organised around the pooling of diverse income sources rather than the formation of family businesses. From the perspective of the 'subsistence' household potential income includes formal wages and casual employment in the informal economy as well as unemployment benefits, sickness benefits, workers' compensation payments and old age pensions. Humphrey (1984) found that there was considerable variation in the sources of income across households from different sectarian communities. Among the older-established Maronite community there was much greater level of wage incomes than among the more recent Sunni community. Thus, while among Maronite households only 32 per cent of all income sources of household members came from welfare and workers' compensation payments, among Sunni households 60 per cent these sources. Similarly, 10 per cent of the more established Maronite households reported incomes from businesses, while among the Sunni only 3 per cent had income of this kind.[67]

In addition to these sources of income, family and community members could call on each other to provide casual unpaid labour to concrete a drive way, help in the building of a house extension, house painting or perhaps moving house. Among the Lebanese refugees urban subsistence strategies were organised around collective income sources from the formal and informal labour market, dependance on the state welfare system and reciprocities based on family and community ties.

The formation of composite households was also a strategy of urban subsistence. As Khuri observes in his Beirut study, '... joint families are social instruments the poor use to accommodate to the economic strains of the suburbs.'[68] However, the internal organisation of such households is characteristically fluid and shaped by the composition of the household and the stage in the domestic cycle. In Sydney composite households were usually formed around the need for childcare in young families and the needs of migrants on arrival.

Childcare needs have played an important role in shaping the composition of households.[69] Frequently grandparents are recruited as dependants under the 'family reunion' immigration category in order to provide childcare. However, filial obligations to care for the aged did not necessarily ensure their status as permanent members of composite households. In wage-based households unemployment can change the equation of need and affordability of additional household members. In these circumstances, grandparents can become an economic burden because they are ineligible for state welfare or pension benefits under the terms of their acceptance as migrants. The Maintenance Guarantee arrangement allows individuals to sponsor parents if they accept financial responsibility for them for ten years.[70]

In family businesses where workplace and residence are a contiguous space – a shop or restaurant – the problem of childcare is simplified. Children are close by and can be employed around the shop doing chores after school and at weekends. In fact the contribution of women and children to the family business is not merely casual, but an essential ingredient for maximising the takings of many family businesses.[71] In such households any additional member, including grandparents, becomes part of the division of labour of the family as a productive household.

The practical problems of adjustment to the new social circumstances of migration and tensions over parental authority can lead to a falling out between parents and children in joint households. This problem is not unique to Lebanese immigrants but is experienced by many different ethnic groups. The Latin American Grandparents' Association formed in 1980, for example, was the first organisation formed to deal precisely with the problem of isolation and poverty experienced by grandparents brought out under the Maintenance Guarantee scheme who had subsequently fallen out with their children.

The other situation where people are most likely to be members of composite households is when they first migrate. One study found that 64 per cent reported that they became members of composite households on arrival in Sydney and that only 24 per cent had remained in joint households at the time of the survey.[72] Chain migration, especially under the circumstances which the Lebanese refugees arrived, located people in households of family and friends, but usually only as a temporary arrangement.

If urban subsistence is the emerging pattern of proletarianisation among immigrants, then the household is the centrepiece of this experience. However, the physical household does not define the limits of reciprocity in migration. Economic co-operation between family households separated by migration takes a variety of forms among Lebanese refugees. More than 50 per cent of all households reported sending remittances on a regular basis to family in Lebanon and in the case of the Sunni almost three-quarters of all households.[73] Other forms of support included sponsorship and assistance for the migration of family members under the 'family reunion' scheme which included becoming guarantor for the basic needs and welfare and arranging marriage between family members to facilitate migration.

Co-operation between family members in Sydney included financial support for the education of a talented nephew or niece or the pooling of savings to buy housing. Some families combined their assets to provide a deposit to secure a housing loan. They would each then take it in turn to purchase a house through the strategy of forming joint households and collective savings.

This description of the experience of Lebanese proletarianisation in Sydney focused on strategies of urban subsistence raises questions about their social futures. In a country of permanent migration like Australia, the myth of generational mobility has sustained high levels of immigration. In reality, social mobility has been closely connected culturally with assimilation to the middle class, even if that has been with outward displays of cultural diversity. However, the urban subsistence strategies described here based on reciprocities and cultures reorganised in migration suggest the reproduction of marginality across generations.

The difference between the circumstances under which earlier immigrants recreated cultural practices and identities, and those under which the Lebanese refugees have recreated family and community life is critical to understanding contemporary processes of proletarianisation internationally. Because governments in the developed world no longer consider 'growth and full employment' achievable through market mechanisms, the political solution has been to increasingly withdraw from the role of mediating between the interests of capital and labour. Instead, they have sought to find ways to define members of the potential labour force as being outside the labour market. Immigrants, married women, older people and youth are the targets of such policies of exclusion which include early retirement schemes, prohibiting the employment of illegal migrants, raising school retention rates, or offering the incentive of subsides for self-employment and small business. This strategy seeks to 'reduce the supply of labour by defining and providing, for certain persons and certain time periods, the conditions of legitimate non-participation in the labour market.'[74] Offe points out that the most attractive alternative is '... the self-supporting family household, which is, therefore, often recommended as the ideal form of 'accommodation ' for women, youth and the elderly, whose labour-power must be prevented from appearing on the market.'[75] However, the family household has a limited capacity to cope with this economic burden. The patterns of part-time or causal employment, participation in the informal sector, unemployment and resort to family businesses are all evidence of the labour market marginalisation of the Lebanese refugee.

Conclusion

The 'refugees' discovered that in Sydney their cultural capital located them in urban space which was undergoing significant changes. The recreation of family and community in the city was an expression of the necessity of social reciprocity. Urban space made them marginal proletarians as long term unemployed and participants in the informal economy and the state reinforced this by a policy which had long focused on social reciprocity as a cheap strategy of settlement. Ties of family, village community and sect were the conduits of support and access to the wider world of the city.

The pluralism of the city was the major locus of social consciousness, rather than the state's ideology of national identity. In fact the state adjusted the nationalist rhetoric of 'White Australia' to correspond to the pluralism of the city where ethnic identity was formed. In Australia the high level of concentration of immigrants in the two major cities of Sydney and Melbourne forged multiculturalism as a city ideology where new identities were forged by communal patterns of settlement and the approved politics of clientism.

In the case of the refugees, these identities were internally differentiated by the generational depth of the Lebanese Christian and Muslim communities and were strongly connected to deep-rooted assumptions of integration and the recreation of peasant cultures. The very embourgeoisement of ethnic cultures, where social differentiation implies desirability, was an integral part of the elaboration of Lebanese Muslim and Christian ethnic histories.

The other dimension of these locality-based cultures was their internationalisation, linked by travel and communication to the social worlds they had left behind. The very articulation of difference drew strongly upon the fragments of Lebanese life as the state itself disintegrated. Lebanese cultural difference was historicised and located in the narratives of Middle East crisis – the problem of nationhood, the persistence of descent-based identity and state violence against the protests of the impoverished and marginalised. The next chapter addresses the cultural roots of this internationalisation of small cultural worlds, the connection of social spaces, and locates it in the experience of nation state.

3

The Lebanese Heritage

The study of immigrant communities always suggests a study of their heritage, the origins of what they brought with them. The significance of heritage is not merely the persistence of cultural frameworks for understanding new lives in migration. It is that migration presents a new context in which social life is created and recreated. Heritage itself, however, is also produced. The familiar ethnographic features of Lebanese society – family, community and sect – have themselves been produced in the context of nation-making and proletarianisation in Lebanon.

The character of family, community and sect as social spaces produced from the experience of pluralism, proletarianisation and the creation of national community in Lebanon is the subject of this chapter. The focus of the discussion is the relationship between the locality, city and nation as sites of social integration and cultural production. Each had its distinct forms of association and integration in Lebanon.

The Lebanese nation enclosed plural cultural forms, but did not succeed in making pluralism a mode of social integration. Instead, Lebanese pluralism was sustained at many levels by the role of clientism in particularising and personalising power throughout Lebanese society, and also by the internationalisation of the social spaces of family, community and sect. The integrity of these cultural forms was sustained by a relationship between the inside and outside worlds. Family structures were internationalised through household remittances, marriage and chain migration, community by maintaining links to the global village in the diaspora, and sect by perpetuating minority religious cultures and networks in the diaspora.

The regional factors which promoted the internationalisation of Lebanese society grew out of the unresolved character of the Lebanese national culture – was it primarily Arab and Muslim in orientation or Christian and Western? The political and cultural movements of the region strongly shaped segments of Lebanese society and their juxtaposed identities. Thus the Arab nationalist ideology, the politics of the Palestinian presence, Islamist movements and Beirut's role as a regional finance, trade and leisure centre all contributed to the internationalisation of Lebanese society.

The creation of the Lebanese nation state had changed the historical relationship between culture and political power, especially between religion and state power. The Lebanese state did not embrace secularism as the basis of the new national community. The reordering of society in the new state drew upon the pre-existing system of Ottoman *millets* – the idea of society constituted as discrete groups – but the political content of cultural pluralism and the politico-legal significance of sect fundamentally changed in the new nation state. The mandatory power made cultural difference the logic of Syrian partition and Lebanese nation-building.

> Emphasising the evident differences between the communities – Maronites, Nusayris, Druzes, Antioch Turks, bedouin – but ignoring their greater fundamental similarities, the French planners could assert that, by their policy, they were merely yielding to the actual facts of heterogeneous Syrian society – were preventing the subordination, perhaps the ill-treatment, of weak by stronger elements, were giving the more backward (or in Lebanon, the more advanced) a better chance of evolution in comparative isolation than they could enjoy as engulfed parts of a Syrian state, and were reserving for them

> a later day of self-determination when they could, if they wished, join the main body'[1]

The pluralism of the Lebanese state was both an expression of the cultural worlds it enclosed and the autonomy the state lacked. Colonial midwifery ensured that the national social order was ultimately guaranteed externally and not internally. The conditions of national independence were in fact a set of dependencies, external guarantees to hold the national enterprise in place. The national bourgeoisie in Lebanon had cosmopolitan tastes and ties. The basis of their command over social space was their shared monopoly over state resources which they used to exercise control over the population by making them clients, not citizens. Their international alliances provided the means to perpetuate social advantage by privileged access to valued international cultural capital – especially education. The working and middle classes were internationally connected through localised worlds of kin and community which provided them with remittances and sometimes opportunities to emigrate.

Both the rich and the poor in Lebanon developed their own internationalised worlds. The former through command over cultural capital which would ensure their privilege, and the latter through remittances and possible emigration which lessened their dependencies on the patronage of the rich and powerful. The rich had the cultural and financial means to enter the ranks of a cosmopolitan world. The not-so-rich generally managed to acquire portable professional and technical qualifications to become labour migrants or emigrants, while the poor fell back on the family as a mode of international subsistence.

What follows is an argument about the internationalised nature of Lebanese social life. Lebanon cannot be understood as a national entity which fragmented through the failure of modernity but an internationalised social space where the relationship between different social classes was mediated by their relationship to outside worlds. Moreover the nature of community in Lebanon created the basis for the internationalisation of locality based society as ethnic communities.

Making the Lebanese Nation State

The nation states of the Middle East were formed by partitioning the territory of the Ottoman Empire. In the process the prevailing Ottoman social order organised around communal pluralism and status hierarchy under Sunni overlordship was either overturned, or radically altered, in the structure of the new nation states. The Turkish nation state itself represented the most radical transformation in the region. A secular state structure was established, Islam was relegated to the domain of private personal belief, and all minority cultures were expected to assimilate to the new Turkish nationalism. Where assimilation was resisted repression and/or expulsion followed. In the early 1920s some 2 million Turks and Greeks were exchanged between Turkey and Greece as part of the enterprise of cultural homogenisation.[2]

Lebanon, by contrast, enshrined the principle of pluralism in the constitution of the new state by institutionalising communalism. Building upon the Ottoman millet system which had granted a degree of autonomy to minority religious communities in matters of personal status, taxation and military conscription, the French extended communal identity as the constitutional basis for membership in the new nation state. In doing so they were following a colonial precedent in Cyprus where the British had made communal identity (Greek and Turkish) the basis for political representation in a legislative assembly in 1882.[3]

In Lebanon, communalism became the vehicle for social engineering in the new state. By careful territorial sculpturing the population enclosed by boundaries yielded a Christian majority thereby inverting the ranking of the previous political order in which Muslim had dominated Christian communities. The Maronite Catholics, with the French Mandate authorities acting as midwife, carved out the Lebanese state from the former Ottoman province of Syria and the Mutesarrifate of Mount Lebanon, the autonomous Maronite Christian district established by the Réglement Organique in 1861. The mutesarrifate itself had been the product of French intervention after the massacres on the Mountain which erupted in the context of significant social and political change in Maronite society on the Mountain.[4] These included the demise of big Maronite landowning families, the growth of priestly power, the dislocation caused by a decade of Egyptian occupation and Ottoman concern over the growth of foreign influence. In the new state political power was distributed amongst 17 officially recognised communal groups thereby guaranteeing Maronite power and reducing the formerly dominant Sunni Muslim community to second position.

The boundaries of the Lebanese state bore little relationship to the former Ottoman provincial boundaries. In 1914 the Ottoman Arab East had been divided into three provinces (Aleppo, Suriyya and Beirut) and three special districts (Lebanon, Dair az-Zur and Jerusalem). The new Greater Lebanon, proclaimed by the French General Gouraud on 31 August 1920, was a littoral state consisting of Mount Lebanon, the urban Sunni Muslim centres of Tyre, Sidon, Beirut and Tripoli, the large estates of the predominantly Sunni Akkar region, the Druze Shuf and the predominantly Shi'i Muslim South Lebanon.[5] The society enclosed by the new boundaries preserved the idea of Lebanon as the historical refuge of persecuted religious minorities in a Sunni dominated Levant.

Political pluralism came with imperialist guarantees. The French viewed their Mandate as an extension of their assumed historical role as protector of the Maronites which dated back to the Crusades.

Evoking the historical memory of the Crusades, General Henri Gouraud dramatically enacted the role of faithful protector in 1920 when he visited the famous tomb of Saladin outside the Ummayyad Mosque soon after arriving in Damascus. On reaching the tomb he is supposed to have knocked on the door and said to its inmate, 'Listen, Saladin, we have returned!'[6] The French saw themselves as the political midwife for the creation of a Maronite-dominated state and its ultimate guarantor.

The distribution of communal power in the new state was based upon a unique population census conducted under the Mandate in 1932. The census established the power sharing balance of 6:5 Christians to Muslims which was translated into a proportional allocation of parliamentary seats amongst the 17 constituent sects. The census confirmed the majority Christian character of the state. Subsequent demographic change was never measured by census, leaving unchallenged the original distribution of power.

The political ramifications of the formal constitutional provisions were spelled out in greater detail in the National Pact of 1943. Although not formally incorporated into the constitution, the National Pact allocated the offices of government according to the confessional proportions established by the 1932 census. In addition the hierarchy of sect was clearly delineated through the allocation of high political office; the presidency was reserved for a Maronite Catholic, the premiership for a Sunni Muslim, and the position of speaker of the house for a Shi'i Muslim.[7]

The historical inversion of communal power that confessionalism represented imposed another constraint on the development of Lebanese national identity. Under the National Pact the Arab nationalists and Francophile Maronites agreed to suspend public debate about the nature of the historical political and cultural ties which shaped Lebanon. For the sake of political harmony the 'Lebanese national story' was put aside.[8] In private, however, the competing versions of the 'Lebanese story' continued to be nurtured by the different sects.

As well as inhibiting the development of national identity, confessionalism also limited the centralisation of state power by leaving largely unchallenged the ties of patronage to regional power holders, the traditional notable families who had long dominated the region's politics. The notable families succeeded in extending their local power to the state arena by virtually monopolising parliamentary seats.[9] Through the electoral system they were able to reinforce local patronage ties by their enhanced access to state resources.

Nor did the new form of social membership, citizenship, provide the means to secure rights independently of the particularism of patronage. Citizenship rights – political, civil and social – were either restricted or mediated by communal institutions. Political representation was mediated by the primary membership of sect, civil rights were delimited by religious jurisdiction over personal law and by the political intervention of the powerful, and social rights were neglected or ceded to powerful religious institutions.

Confessionalism allowed the political elite to retain influence over their constituencies by restricting citizenship rights to the descendants of the sectarian communities. Descent and sect endogamy were used to retain their share of political power. The balance of communal power was such a sensitive issue that applications for citizenship from immigrants, refugees and their descendants from other parts of the Middle East were almost always denied. As one Lebanese born Palestinian observed: 'We speak the same language, have the same culture and religion and they call us refugees.' The religious monopoly over personal law – there was no civil law of marriage, divorce or inheritance – also created the legal means to enforce sect endogamy overseen by the religious establishment.

Clientism rather than nationalism was the primary mode of incorporation in the state. In the Mediterranean these have been the competing modes of membership in the modern state. Whereas clientism '... represents a vertical mode of cohesion among unequals, nationalism '... represents a horizontal mode of cohesion, theoretically at least, among equals.'[10] In clientalist politics communal inequality was addressed by conferring individual benefit.

Clientism was one way of trying to regulate demands created by proletarianisation. Another was to allow private institutions to assume responsibility for areas such as health, education and welfare that the state could not provide.

In the area of education the state took the lead from French colonial policy which had dismantled the existing Ottoman public primary school system.[11] Within five years of receiving the mandate, the number of students attending state primary schools was halved in preference for enrolment in the new French schools. The medium of instruction of both the state and French systems was French. However, despite insistence on secularism at home, the French failed to develop any state secondary schools at all. This policy of neglect, and the introduction of French as a *langue vivante*, produced an educational system which by the 1960s and 1970s had become socially elitist, culturally divided along sectarian lines and infused with an entrepreneurial and commercial spirit.

Arabic language state schools ranked a poor last in both status and educational quality in Lebanon. The Arabic language universities could not compete with internationally sponsored and connected institutions such as the long-established American University of Beirut which taught in English and the Jesuit St Joseph University which taught in French. The languages of prestige and opportunity remained the languages of the old colonial powers of the Middle East. The AUB itself was used by the US government as an institution of cultural co-option through a system of scholarships for promising students from the Third World.

Nor was the Lebanese state able to protect the growing urban proletariat by regulating the labour market or providing welfare services through an effective taxation system. The chronic inadequacy of wage incomes for many families was managed by maintaining subsistence strategies between the city and village. By allowing the growth of the informal sector the state expanded employment but created the conditions of low-income urban subsistence. The lifestyles of urban middle class benefited through cheap services, but the urban poor remained trapped.

Making the Lebanese: Proletarianisation and Pluralism

While confessionalism was the new basis for political membership proletarianisation reshaped the social consciousness of sect in the new state. The economic mobilisation of Lebanese had begun in the mid-nineteenth century and took two main forms. The first was their entry into commercial agriculture and cash cropping, and the second was participation in labour migration, internal rural– urban migration as well as international migration.

In traditional Ottoman society sect had been a social marker which conferred rank in the cultural hierarchy. The relationship between religion and occupation, while not definitive, was often suggestive. Thus in Lebanon the majority of Lebanese Shi'is and Druze were peasants and often tenants to feudal landowners; the majority of Sunnis resided in the towns and cities and were employed as artisans, shopkeepers and in services; while the majority of Maronites were peasants, often smallholders.

A series of peasant rebellions in the nineteenth century marked the beginning of the proletarianisation of the peasantry. Rebellion against Ottoman taxation or local overlords saw the breakdown of the land owning structures, but not of Ottoman control of the countryside. The Maronite peasantry, in alliance with the clergy, rebelled against the Druze Khazin overlords in the 1858 Kisrawan uprisings and 1889 the Druze rose against the Atrash lords.[12]

One outcome of the 1860 rebellions was Ottoman reform of land tenure from usufruct to private ownership in land which brought considerable change to rural society. The Ottoman appointment of official tax collectors under the 1861 Tanzimat reforms had the effect of reducing the big landowning families share of the Mountain's wealth from 75 per cent to 10 per cent by the early 1900s. The system of tax-farmers was replaced by a new class of urban-based absentee landowners in Syria and Lebanon.[13]

Land reform and political change introduced new economies into which the Maronite peasantry were quickly drawn. Originally dominated by the big landowning families, the political economy of Mount Lebanon was transformed in the mid-nineteenth century by the expansion of the silk trade and associated artisan crafts, the penetration of European commodities and the expansion of usury relations.[14] The close historical and cultural ties of the Maronites with France facilitated French investment in sericulture which drew mainly upon Maronite labour and skills. Political as well as economic developments contributed to the differential proletarianisation across the sects.

When the French assumed control under the Mandate the broad outlines of the Mountain's economy were already beginning to emerge. There was a weak and limited manufacturing sphere and a backward agriculture where a majority of small holders lived either in debt or heavily dependant upon remittances from emigré relatives. Capital resources were invested in largely non-productive areas, such as import/export transit and retail trade, rental property and real estate in Beirut, hotels, tourism, and land speculation in the Lebanese Mountains. Tourism had began to develop before 1914, promoted and funded by '... the nostalgic propaganda of prosperous Syrians abroad'.[15] Mandatory agencies abroad greatly expanded tourism and *estivage* (summer holidaying) by foreign visitors through hotel and road development and by 1939 tourism had reached 16,000 tourists, 19,000 *estivants* and 1,000 (foreign skiers).[16]

Emigration was the other major social impact of the economic and political changes which began in Mount Lebanon. Ottoman attempts to modernise and to retain political power through greater centralisation were seen as repression and victimisation by the Maronites and other religious minorities. This led to a large-scale exodus of population, principally to the Americas, and to their proletarianisation through labour migration. Emigration had been officially prohibited by the Ottoman's until 1896 when the policy was changed because of the evident economic benefits of remittances. By 1919 the level of remittances from the Americas represented over 40 per cent of the income of the Ottoman Mutessarifate of Mount Lebanon.[17] The fear of the loss of skilled labour and a general population drain also proved to be unfounded. A large proportion of the Syrian–Lebanese emigrants to the Americas returned home bringing their savings with them.[18]

The family-based banks, which were later to emerge as an important service industry, drew heavily upon the remittances of emigrants. Banking, insurance and credit had been dominated by European agencies such as the (Anglo–French) Imperial Ottoman Bank and the Crédit Lyonnais.

The French Mandate also opened up colonial opportunities for migrants, particularly in West Africa, in petty commerce and trading. Maronite and Shi'i emigrants became the most prominent commercial communities in the French colonies and retained this position in the post-colonial era.

The urbanisation of Beirut was the other major force in Lebanese proletarianisation. The city's role as a mercantile port and later, in 1888, administrative capital of a new Ottoman *wilaya* made it a natural choice as the administrative headquarters of the French mandate. The French administration made the modernisation of Beirut a high priority resulting in a rapid growth in investment, construction and population. From 1921–32 the population doubled to 161,382.[19] However, by focusing on urban development at the expense of the rural areas and population, '... the Mandate Authority helped to precipitate massive migration to an unprepared city, and the concomitant social and political problems.'[20]

In the 1950s urbanisation was the major force in Lebanese proletarianisation. The emergence of Beirut as a regional entrepot, finance and leisure centre created an economic boom focused on services and construction.[21] The resulting investment and urban growth stimulated an enormous rural–urban migration which led to almost half the national population, 1.5 million, living in Beirut by the mid-1970s. The internationalising of Beirut transformed the whole countryside into its social hinterland. In the city itself internationalised urban space, represented by banking, finance and tourism, existed alongside subsistence rural immigrant communities whose labour serviced their lifestyles and investments.

The city not only dominated the countryside but was the main site where the political and material realities of sectarian difference were learned by a new urban population. Community identity was forged in the new proletarian world of the city. Migration politicised sect setting cheek by jowl communities whose social worlds had been previously separated by geography and history. Sectarian difference was marked off in the city by an urban topography of affluence and poverty and by the retention of sectarian patronage channels.

Proletarianisation took place through rural–urban migration but this did not generally result in the detachment of rural from urban society. Immigrants to the city provided the social conduit for access to housing and jobs for relatives and friends coming from the village. The village remained a focus of social obligation, subsistence and political connection in the patronage system for those in the city. New communities and social identities in the city were constructed out of the cultural capital transplanted from the village. This was reflected spatially in the residential concentrations based on sect and village, especially in the newer suburbs. The famous 'Belt of Misery' in the southern suburbs of Beirut which Imam Moussa Sadr made his political constituency in the early 1970s was inhabited mainly by Shi'i villagers from South Lebanon.

The formation of urban village 'communities' was not simply a reconstruction of the village in the city – an expression of the continuity of the same cultural consciousness. The reliance on family and community ties in the city was more significantly a political strategy of the poor to gain control over social space in the city. As Harvey argues, the capacity of the poor to control urban space depends upon their '... continuous appropriation' of it, intensive transactions in small personalised social worlds.[22] Community is created through ' ... mutual aid and mutual predation, creating tight but often highly conflictual interpersonal social bonding in both private and public spaces.'[23] Control is exercised within this social world through cultural differentiation using '... fine-tuned ethnic, racial and status discriminations'.[24]

In the city the social relations of the neighbourhood, and not the workplace, were the main locus of the culture of proletarianisation. Incorporation was not mediated through working class labour organisations, the organisation of labour against capital, but through the social relations of community and its relationship to the wider urban world.

The social contiguity of urban and rural space was apparent in immigrant household organisation. The significance of kin ties was actually enhanced through migration and social mobility, even for those remaining in the village. People organised their lives and their obligations between the households in the village and suburb. Farsoun describes these dispersed households as the 'functionally extended family' performing all the same functions as the 'classical' nucleated extended family.[25] Khuri (1975) found that family organisation in rural–urban migration emphasised the continued importance of consanguinal ties on settlement patterns, occupational structure, investment and capital formation, economic aid, household organisation and marriage and divorce.

The formation of nuclear households in the city also had to be understood in terms of the contiguity of the urban–rural space. Nuclear households amongst South Lebanese rural–urban immigrants, for example, indicated a higher level of affluence but it also concealed the fact that they tended to support more kin in the village. As Khuri summarises: '... as people migrate or become rich, they tend to support more kin while they reside with less kin'.[26] The presence of extended households in the city, by contrast, reflected their relative poverty.

These subsistence strategies of household organisation were not continuous with traditional forms but rather new forms adapted to the city. 'People do not only gather more dependents as they migrate, generating a higher rate of unemployment in the countryside, but also create new household organisation in order to accommodate for the economic pressures of the suburbs'.[27]

Family constituted a social network that was not merely an expression of the continuity of rurality, but the basis for 'urban subsistence' in the city. It was an element in the constitution of community as well as the medium through which many entered the urban economy. The family was the focus of economic activity – if not an economic unit – across all classes in the city. Manufacturing, retail stores and commercial enterprises were predominantly family firms.[28] Also partnerships and corporations were generally partnerships of siblings, cousins or other extended kin and very often corporations were nothing more than legal protection for wholly family-owned or extended kin-owned establishments. Recruitment of migrants into wage labour also relied upon kin connections. Family dependence rather than class based collective bargaining was the primary mode of economic security.

The division of households by emigration often overturned the patriarchal structures of day to day life, especially in the village. The act of emigration by men made women heads of households. As a result of the war the significance of women remaining in the village changed. Traditionally the women who remained in the village to wait were seen as the symbol of continuity with the land and family life. Cooke points out that during the war staying in the village became an act of caring, curing and nurturing in a collapsing society.[29] The male assertiveness of going out, of emigration, became an act of abandonment.

Family ties between the village and the city also provided the basis for organising clienteles and mobilising political support in the city. Voluntary associations, family associations, clubs and political gangs all grew out of the residential clustering of families around village of origin and sectarian community. Genealogy was explicitly used in 'family associations'. These represented new forms of lineage mobilisation in the city among people whose family status traditionally had little political standing. The emergence of family associations brought new relevance to genealogy as a system of family recruitment for specific political ends.

In local municipal elections, factional alignments and national elections support was mobilised through the family. The heads of families or family associations were solicited to deliver votes in elections and to provide support for local za'im (boss) as political gang members. Households, lineage associations and village factions were the basis for electoral success and the exercise of local power on the street. Women generally played no role in this political arena.

Sect was the incorporating ideology beyond family. The confessional system enforced sect consciousness at the electoral level and patronage fixed political attachment to one's village. Thus just as the political economy of household organisation reinforced the social connection between village and city so too did electoral politics. Birthplace and not residence determined electoral registration and therefore the attachment to political clienteles. Consequently immigrants to the city, overwhelmingly of the first generation, remained politically connected to their village constituencies, even though they might have lived in the city for a decade or more. While it was legally possible to change one's electoral registration it was difficult in practice since deputies were reluctant to see their constituencies decline.[30] Clientism reinforced localism and social origin by emphasising communal attachments and identities despite the large scale relocation of population to Beirut. Locality and descent continued to define the social world even in the city.

In the city itself the urban political process saw political bosses (*zu'ama*) manipulate clienteles through the use of family ties. Because the state was distant the family remained the focus of security for its members. The capacity of political bosses to channel patronage to their clientele determined their political success over their rivals. The state was used as a resource for patronage to influence the electorate through the family as a client nexus.[31] The recruitment of client families was seen as an enduring arrangement which was expected to continue patrilineally from father to son.[32]

Within the suburbs alternative political structures emerged which, while focused on family, were not connected to the traditional confessional clientalist structures. Joseph (1982) describes the family amongst the urban proletariat as being a focus for co-option and coercion. In the absence of a social wage provided by the state various radical political parties sought support amongst the urban poor along similar lines to the political gangs. Bourj Hammoud in the early 1970s was an example of a culturally diverse population which had little allegiance to the state. This fragmented urban space instead became the recruiting ground for political parties, movements and militias which had no representation in government. In fact their allegiances frequently brought them into conflict with the state. The proximity of two large Palestinian camps, Tal al-Zatar and Jisr al-Pasha saw conflict overflow into Bourj Hammoud where the Palestinians had allies and enemies.[33]

The state provided the framework for social differentiation and the *zu'ama* ensured their clientele thought in terms of dependency through family ties. This was the dominant model of political recruitment and dependence which political movements outside the state also emulated. The incorporation of the new urban working class was pursued by exploiting their own strategies of security. As Joseph (1982) argues, this became a source of security, but also political bondage locking them into their class position.

In Beirut 'urban subsistence' was constructed around the family and village network and was mutually exploited by both the political bosses and families.

Religion and the Lebanese State

The formation of Lebanon was premised upon a radical inversion of the relationship between religion and power in Ottoman society. Sunni Islam was relegated from the religion of power and privilege to second rank in a multi-religious society. Religion mediated the relationship between the individual and state, making membership of the religious prior to membership of the political community. Religion, instead of legitimating political rule as it had done under the Ottoman system, enforced sect endogamy within a competitive confessional structure. Sect was an index of status in the religious hierarchy and the primary social cleavage along which political patronage flowed.

Constitutionally the state ceded particular areas of social regulation to religion. The most important was the exclusive jurisdiction granted to the religious courts over matters of marriage, divorce and inheritance. The absence of any civil jurisdiction served to enforce sect endogamy. Cross sect marriages necessitated either the conversion of one party or marriage under civil law in another country – most commonly Cyprus.

The concession of exclusive religious jurisdiction over personal status was a source of political tension in the early 1950s between the secular legal system and the religious establishment. The Lebanese legal profession went on strike for three months in 1952 over the government's refusal to present a bill providing for a civil code of personal law for all Lebanese. The compromise which proposed a choice between religious and secular personal law jurisdiction was defeated by religious leaders who called for a general strike which closed down the markets. The status quo prevailed, personal status law remained within the jurisdiction of the religious courts.

Through its legal concessions to religious authority, the state endorsed a strongly patriarchal family structure. Under religious law men had considerable legal power over women and over property. Inheritance and the allocation of the custody of children and family property in divorce across all religious groups upheld patrilineal family structures. In the early 1970s family law in Lebanon was described as 'wearing a moustache'.[34]

The legal subordination of women was reinforced by the ideology of honour which trapped them in a closely regulated social world. Honour commodified women as objects for exchange in the marriage market. Men assumed responsibility for the sexual supervision of women to ensure their marriage value and family honour was not jeopardised. Family concerns about marital security were expressed in the legal contract of marriage. The amount specified for bridewealth (*al-mahr*) – the immediate and deferred payment expressed in the marriage contract – varied with the kin proximity of the couple. This was traditionally larger for an out-marriage than an in-marriage, as the latter was considered more secure.

In the new state religious institutions continued to play a role in articulating political power. In Ottoman times the political elite had controlled the religious institutions and monopolised the use of religious symbols. The *millet* system had conferred official status on minority religious institutions and placed them in political hierarchy of influence. Religion was employed politically as a socially incorporating and regulating institution between sectarian communities and the state.

In the countryside in north Lebanon religion had been integrated into the local system of domination over the Sunni peasantry creating a symbiotic relationship between beys (landlords) and local shaikhs. The bey's exercise of political power over peoples lives was experienced directly, largely unmediated by geography or institutional mechanisms. The shaikhs in this schema played the ambiguous role of reproducing the local social system in their interests and those of the beys as well as presenting themselves as a foil to the bey. In popular belief shaikhs could resist the power of the beys by their ability to perform miracles to protect the powerless and poor – those the landlords oppressed.[35] The religious standing and power of the shaikh '... was produced by the "respectful" gifts of the lord.'[36]

In the city the relationship between the Sunni notables and the religious establishment was also close. In the Mandate period for example, 'Abdel Hamid Karami, a member of a leading Tripolitan family, held in turn the posts of Mufti of Tripoli and Premier of Lebanon. Forms of religious adherence also functioned as symbolic markers of status difference in Tripoli. Hence leading families followed the Shafi'i school while tradesmen's families followed the Maliki school.[37] Senior religious officials also played an intermediary role in the administration of welfare subsidised by the political elite.[38]

In Lebanese confessional politics control over key Muslim institutions was not only an important source of patronage but also central to power-broking in the appointment of prime minister, a Sunni office under the constitution. Within the city Muslim charitable organisations provided an avenue for patronage and power-broking between the parliamentary deputies and the street. The Sunni Maqassad (Benevolent Society) in Beirut, for example, provided a large range of educational and health services which could be allocated as patronage. Conflicts within these institutions had the potential to expand to become national political crises. The presidency of the Maqassad played a pivotal role in the selection of candidates for the premiership.[39]

In Lebanon clientism and religious pluralism were politically articulated. The multiplicity of locality was conceptually linked by religious membership (the imagined community) and politically connected through clientism. Sect in this structure became the means of defining and reproducing the accepted channels of influence and distribution of power.

Proletarianisation in the city did not rupture the ties of locality because the family and community, not the workplace, remained the primary locus of urban incorporation. The boundaries between urban spaces were defined in cultural terms, usually sect. With the movement of the population to the city sect was no longer a geographically dispersed but a concentrated category, marking off urban differences with clearly delineated channels to the political centre.

Unmaking Lebanon: Civil War and Localism

War laid bare the fragility of the social and political fabric of the Lebanese nation state. The response to state collapse was fragmentation and social contraction. All the institutions mediating the relationship between the state and the population either dissolved or became largely irrelevant in the face of power seized locally by the gun. The political elite lost control of their sources of patronage in the state and the influence of senior religious officials waned.

Local power holders replaced their former bosses, taking command of the street with their militias. As violence overran suburbs, towns and villages the links between people, inside and outside Lebanon, were revealed as they fled. Social spaces became increasingly homogenised as the practice of sectarian killing – now called 'ethnic cleansing' after the disintegration of Yugoslavia – undermined any basis of social trust other than communalism. Terror helped define boundaries and enclose co-religionists tying them to the same political project. The war also collapsed the distinction between rural and urban space. 'Beirut and the village were identified in such a way that the village had become a microcosm for Lebanon.'[40]

The 'Green Line' in Beirut symbolised the shattering of confessionalism and its replacement by cantonisation, the break-up of Lebanon into small worlds. These worlds, however, could not survive as relatively autonomous domains without international connections and support. Urban subsistence came in all forms; families, village communities, states, political parties, and radical political movements. Violence forged identity and dependency. Those who could not remain self-sufficient through reliance on family, wages and remittances were inevitably drawn into the war through protection and predation. The victims of war, the refugees and dispossessed, were forced into the arms of those who sought to coral people into the new sectarian and militia constituencies.

The war not only revealed the fragmented nature of Lebanese society but also the depth of its internationalisation. Capital fled the centrepiece of the Lebanese economy, tourism and finance. The wealthy could retreat to metropolitan capitals where many had homes and investments or they could easily establish a temporary life. The flight of the middle and working classes to visit or settle with families and communities in other countries was an indication of the depth of generational emigration in the population as a whole. But the most important indication of its internationalisation was the growing dependence on a remittance economy. Life was sustained by incomes from outside the country – males who had undertaken temporary labour migration, family members who had settled permanently in another country.

On the political front the struggle for control of the streets became dependent on the financial sponsorship of external backers rather than the patronage of national politicians. The fragmentation of national territory was facilitated by the internationalisation of the war. Increasingly social space was enclosed by communal leaders whose power was underwritten by external resources and internally by exclusionist communalism.

Johnson describes this process as the de-secularisation of politics: '... by 1985 the leaders of most of the militias were being sucked into the sectarian discourse of their clienteles.'[41] But radical communalism had other consequences. Islam shifted from being a confessional medium to a medium for radical reinterpretation of social life in Lebanon. The anarchy created by destruction created denationalised space in which new internationalist Islamist movements found fertile ground. The emergence to prominence of both Shi'i and Sunni radical movements after the Israeli invasion of 1982 highlighted the extent to which the old national order had been eclipsed. The Shi'i movement, Hizbollah, seized control of much of West Beirut totally overwhelming the former Sunni political dominance in the city. By taking of Western hostages they sought to delineate new boundaries of an autonomous Islamic domain in the international city. They achieved their aim in 1986 when the remaining Western residents and institutions evacuated the area in response to the escalation of kidnappings and murders.

The Tawhid al-Harakat al-Islamiya (Islamic Unification Movement), a Sunni radical movement which seized control in Tripoli between 1983–86 by expelling the former secularist Arab nationalist and communist parties, was also an expression of new popular forces coming to power in the political vacuum. The local Sunni clerics became agents instead of brokers of power as the political influence of the traditional religious hierarchy in the city declined.[42] Its military character and the ecumenical stance expressed in its leaders' public identification with the Iranian Islamic Revolution was a radical departure from the close alliance of the Sunni establishment with the traditional political elite. The emergence of Tawhid was yet further evidence of the decline of the Sunni community in the confessional equation. Unlike the other confessions they failed to develop a communal consciousness in the war having historically drawn upon the secular inspiration of Arab nationalism.[43] Eventually they were deposed when Syria decided to take direct control of the whole of North Lebanon. The fighting, however, was not carried out by the Syrian army but a pro-Syrian alliance of secular militias.

The war reinforced locality and autonomy in Lebanese social life. The outbreak of fighting saw the city fragment along sectarian and village cleavages. The armed defence of neighbourhoods drew largely on communal attachments in the city or, especially in the early stages of the war, in their home villages. Social spaces became increasingly homogenised by the politics of communal terror as people responded to the arbitrariness of the fighting, shelling and bombing by retreat, either to their neighbourhood or village, or emigration.

The internationalisation of family life increased rapidly through labour migration and emigration. Mobility externally may have remained primarily male, but internally it became feminised. Women writers on the war comment on the importance of women's role in a society that was collapsing.[44] While men often became immobilised by the war because they feared the possibility of mistaken identity, being taken hostage or being murdered as they crossed communal spaces, women were still able to move around maintaining connections with kin all over Lebanon. Even overseas Lebanese families would regularly visit, without their husbands. The men stayed safe in their emigré home.

Conclusion

If the internationalisation of labour migration has led to the pluralisation of cities of the North, its corollary is the multiplication of the locations of dependency of communities in the South. If immigrant families construct new reciprocities across geographically vast distances and new kinds of community are forged out of the processes of urban differentiation and entrapment in these cities of the North, then the South too is being internationalised and fragmented as a consequence. Such internationalisation is taking place not through the investment of capital and the creation of internationalised urban space alongside urban subsistence, but through the internationalisation of connected proletarian ethnic spaces.

The Lebanese heritage has been the experience of a state in which kinship, community and sect have mediated relationships to the new worlds created out of large scale urbanisation. The idiom of kinship was adopted to establish connections (*wasta*), personalise encounters with bureaucracy and government and mobilise family members in clientalist politics.

The heritage of Lebanese immigrants to Australia has been the adaptations of cultural idioms to the experience of the nation and proletarianisation in situations where wage incomes were largely inadequate and the household remained the focus of subsistence. Lebanese migrants to Australia did not bring customs and traditions as blueprints for the reproduction of social life but specific cultural knowledge shaped by the lived experience and application of this knowledge to their particular experience of modernity: of becoming wage labourers, of dividing your family between city and village, of seeking to personalise transactions with powerful institutions, of finding wage incomes inadequate, of citizenship being mediated by sectarian identity and of conceptualising a social world which is geographically dispersed but nevertheless still incurs obligations and benefits. It is also the experience of the disintegration of a national project through civil war and the development of new forms of urban subsistence. The Lebanese 'story' and its legacy is a potential template for the history of many small states and people in the South.

We will now turn back to the North and explore the new frontier of social consciousness in the contemporary world, the multicultural city. In the following chapters the symbolic regulation of social space will be considered in detail. The first focuses on the family and the second on community, both key forms of social consciousness in the immigrant world.

4

Lebanese Families

Migration is always a threat to family life. (Shi'i father in Sydney)

Immigrants have both material contexts and symbolic resources. However, the suggestion that the symbolic can somehow achieve independence from the material is an illusion nurtured in the idea that separate identity constitutes the basis for social autonomy. In this chapter and the next we will look at the question of the relationship between cultural production and social space, focusing first on the family and then on the community as spaces of cultural production. The central issue is how and why cultural practices are generated and sustained in immigrant lives. The central themes are autonomy and dependence, choice and reciprocity.

The urban space of the Lebanese Muslim refugees is constituted through 'relations of personal dependence', earlier described as the direct appropriation of social space by those unable to command space in other ways. Family and community provide the social basis for the occupation of urban space and the symbolic resources for cultural regeneration. The Lebanese Muslim refugees find themselves in a similar situation to that of traditional societies whose frameworks for social organisation, social legitimacy and utility must be constantly renewed and asserted: '... [individuals] have to work directly, daily, personally, to produce and reproduce the conditions of domination which are even then never entirely trustworthy.'[1] Rural emigrants to the city are armed with traditions torn from the social environment which forged them and in which they had lived their lives.

As Bourdieu observes of rural emigrants in Algeria:

> The break with tradition brought about by emigration, the relaxing of collective pressure linked to the anonymity of urban life, contact with a technical civilisation entirely devoted to profane ends the explicit and diffuse teachings of the school, all these influences combine to produce a thorough transmutation of values and to destroy the soil in which traditional religiosity was rooted.[2]

The network of obligations created constitutes the basis of social regulation. It derives from such practices as maintaining collective kin obligations, inculcating filial duty, valuing honour, arranging the marriage of a daughter, ensuring sexual segregation, giving, visiting, performing rituals, doing favours and creating political or economic debts. The self-regulation of community affairs is dependent upon willing mediators, the acceptance of self-help in certain situations, and the possibility of social expulsion.

The centrepiece of obligation and social regulation in immigrant life is the domestic space of the family. Detachment from community of origin, the demands of reciprocity as a strategy for survival, and the urban process of the industrial city make the regulation of domestic space a central feature of settlement. The possibilities of regulation of domestic space centre on symbolic control and personal dependence, the antithesis of individualism and choice. However, for the refugees neither the material nor symbolic conditions for the regeneration of cultural practices are stable. Their attempts to realise imagined worlds (their reconstituted habitus) in the city as the product of their autonomous acts are challenged by other symbolic orders, as well as by material conditions. Youth culture, feminism, racism and the legal system all challenge Muslim immigrant practice, along with low wages and unemployment.

Yet it is misleading to juxtapose immigrant regulation of domestic space as if it were no longer of concern in Western industrial society. The ideal of family life is organised around a 'love and money axis', the combination of happy intimate relationships and material affluence.[3] In this model consumerism and mass entertainment are centred on family life. But without affluence and the cultural orientation towards the same social world of consumer distinction, the focus on internal regulation is defensive.

The organisation of Muslim immigrant social life, its boundaries and spheres of control, are revealed in conflicts over the creation, maintenance and dissolution of social ties. Muslim immigrant family disputes are about cultural production – ties, values, asymmetrical gender relations – and adaptations to patterns of socialisation in urban space. Disputes map out the impact of the urban process in allocating to immigrants certain kinds of social space and the autonomy agents seek to assert through the observance of cultural codes.

But disputes are not merely illustrative, they are also creative. They take the form of narratives testing cultural legitimacy, and thereby reconstituting it. A dispute is a disagreement or quarrel which cannot be resolved privately and so has been made public by one or both of the parties concerned. It involves a claim which is formulated in terms of norms.[4] Such claims either anticipate and accept established settlement norms, procedures and structures, or reject them and propose others.

Disputes are distinctive kinds of social phenomena because implicit within their forms are a complex web of interests, demands and expectations. A dispute not only involves the interests of parties but, during its course, normative and procedural rules are invoked, the source of cultural authority is identified, the relevant public is delimited and the range of possible sanctions articulated.

A dispute reveals the regulatory mechanisms in a particular social space and also, through its history, the relationship between competing regulatory domains. It juxtaposes different forms of narratives whose cultural legitimacy is realised in distinct and separate ways.

A claim is a demand that someone do something, in other words a 'strategy of power'.[5] It invokes models for social behaviour, but it is also a mode of representation. Social relations are represented in normative terms to express order, regularity and continuity, and as a way of organising and controlling them. A claim 'to be in the right' is what Bourdieu calls an 'officialising strategy': '... the object of which is to transmute egoistic, private, particular interests ... into disinterested, collective, publicly avowable, legitimate interests.'[6] By representing the issues in normative terms one invokes the authority of the rules and the means of enforcing compliance, thereby conferring legitimacy on them.

However, the authority of cultural rules is institutionally much less determined in the lives of Lebanese Muslim immigrants because of the nature of the urban space they inhabit. Consequently, disputes assume a narrative form which articulates what is culturally legitimate and interprets and validate rules through a process of community consensus: the accrual of narratives, stories about transgressions and consequences, forms the consensus – or one might say 'Muslim immigrant tradition'.[7]

Narratives are constructed around different armatures of social life, with themes such as kinship obligations, justice, status, authority, love, trust and betrayal. They address collective knowledge whose referents are embedded in a social world to which the whole community has access and they can be constructed around different themes; for example the spatial and temporal context of behaviour or kinship models.

Bourdieu points out that, in North African Muslim tribal society, a small number of generative principles based on pairs provide the basis upon which the seriousness of criminal behaviour can be assessed. Theft is considered more serious, and attracts a more severe penalty, if the first of the following oppositional pairs applies:

house (mosque)/other places
night/day
feast/ordinary day

Similarly homicides are assessed according to the social situation of the victim:

social status: high/low
marital status: married/unmarried
sex: female/male
age: child/adult
weapon: gun/stick
defence: unarmed/armed

Genealogical models are also employed as the basis for determining obligation in deciding on the choice of marriage partner or who should support an individual in a dispute with someone from the same family, lineage or another village.

In these cases, cultural practice is the common property of the community; the ability to decide its authenticity and meaning in a particular instance is not monopolised by a group of specialists. While some individuals' opinions are considered of greater value because of their prestige, learning, age or sex, such people are not usually in a position to impose a decision or act as adjudicator. The 'cyclical process' of negotiation, in which information is exchanged between parties and through which the contending issues and differing accounts are canvassed in the community, establishes, over time, the legitimacy of claims as well as which rules and interpretations apply.

Rules are not merely open to interpretation but are often conditional on the fulfillment of certain standards of reasonable behaviour. For example, in honour disputes in a northern Lebanese village a consistently unreasonable behaviour can lead to an individual being ignored in situations which would normally demand retaliation. Gilsenan (1976) describes this as a process of social anonymisation. Individuals who insist on pressing every point of honour are defined as *makhlu'*, reckless, mad, asocial, dislocated, by members of the wider family. Their behaviour, no matter how provocative, does not demand a response and in fact socially validates non-response. The shame lies in making a response.[8]

Disputes also have the narrative quality of representation. A claim to have acted according to norms can also be calculated to further self-interest. Bourdieu describes such behaviour as 'a second order strategy', one '... whose purpose is to give apparent satisfaction to the demands of the official rule, and thus to compound the satisfactions of enlightened self-interest with the advantage of ethical impeccability.'[9] In this way a disputant represents his/her interest as the general interest.

Kinship Practices

Kinship models have long been the anthropological centrepiece in the study of social life. This is because biological reproduction provides societies with a living map from which to generate models of social regulation through defining actual or fictive relations as the basis for constructing sociality and order. The asymmetry of gender relations has always been central to social ordering through kinship. With biological reproduction as the keystone, control over women's sexuality was made the basis of men's power in the social world. Chastity became the currency for the valuation of women in the marriage market, the exchange of women between consanguinal groups.

In Islam patrilineality became sanctified and codified in religious law. The regulation of sexuality was explicitly made the core of religious morality. While historically this represented the legal regularisation of rights, especially for women, it consolidated the patriarchal basis of society in the transfer of wealth and exercise of power. In Islamic law the subordinate position of women within patrilineal structures is spelled out in the differential rights and capacities of women in the inheritance of wealth, legal witnessing, the capacity to divorce, and the right to guardianship of children.

The sensitivity of gender relations in Islamic culture is not just a political question of male domination, but also derives from the extent to which male and female identity are juxtaposed. Massell, in a study of the new Soviet state's attempt to change the social position of Muslim women in Central Asia, observes that male roles were to an extraordinary extent '... negatively defined with respect to the very concept of woman'.[10] Consequently, the radical policies designed to challenge gender roles threatened '... to dissolve the boundaries defining maleness itself, and hence not just a man's superordinate position vis-à-vis women, but in effect his moral self-image, self-definition, self-esteem and ego-identity.'[11]

In migration the cultural sensitivity of male-female relations becomes particularly acute as social ties contract around the nuclear household. Removed from an environment in which degrees of social distance could be differentiated and regulated by kinship, marriage, family standing and membership of a religious community, gender is recast as a confrontation between the inside/outside, the familiar/foreign and the safe/dangerous in an alien social environment. In this context a gender ideology which celebrates modesty, privacy, dependence and obedience seeks to enclose women within a socially narrowed arena. They are the object of male 'protection' and the vehicle through which the moral preservation of the family is secured or lost.

In migration, kinship models are made central to the regulation of domestic space. Lebanese Muslim immigrant appropriation of urban space – settlement by commanding space through ghettoisation – is focused on the family. In the absence of a strong Muslim cultural and institutional environment, the family assumes the burden of cultural reproduction. Muslim immigrants are no longer socialised by a culturally supportive 'habitus', but have to create one in the family which is frequently reduced to household members alone. One reason for the conservatism of immigrants is found in the intensification of symbolic regulation in the family.

The contraction of the social space available for the maintenance of cultural practices (tradition) to the family has political consequences. Gender asymmetries become exaggerated as men gain greater control over domestic space through social isolation and the growth of local cultural autonomy. Public institutions that historically evolved to intervene in the domestic sphere, especially the incorporating and centralising legal and political institutions of the nation state, are absent (or at least distant) and the new ones (Australian law and society) are unfamiliar, avoided or resisted.

The enhanced authority of men in domestic space in the immigrant community is parallelled by their pre-eminent role in settlement and community formation. Community is constructed from the extension of paternal authority into the community space. Leadership of community associations, the building of mosques, publishing newspapers, business enterprise and ethnic representation are overwhelmingly the worlds of men. The occupation of urban space by the formation of personalised social worlds, small worlds in the city, is primarily the enterprise of men.

Two cultural codes are drawn upon to order Muslim domestic life; Islamic law (the *Shari'a*) and the honour code. Both enhance patriarchal authority in the immigrant family. The former details the prerogatives of male authority in domestic life and the latter attaches patriarchal performance to community status. Islamic law underwrites the prior interest of the patrilineal consanguinal group over conjugal ties in marriage, divorce and inheritance, while honour assumes that women are sexually less responsible and less concerned with family standing. In honour, men's regulation of women is a measure of their social standing. According to men, social order requires them to assume responsibility for women to prevent social chaos.

The core of Muslim family disputes involves gender relations – the ownership of material property, possession of children, regulation of sexuality and domestic authority. Islamic law assumes the social responsibility of men over children and women who are treated as if they were minors: women cannot provide witness in criminal cases, they are entitled to inherit only half that of their brothers, they cannot divorce without the permission of their husband or an Islamic judge. And in divorce their husbands have prior claims to custody of children once they approach puberty.

Culturally. disputes are most frequently expressed as conflicts over the sexual division of labour (domestic confinement, employment, obedience and violence), over the sexual propriety of women (their clothing, male friendships, chastity and fidelity) and over the formation and dissolution of marriage (age of marriage, selection of marriage partner, *al mahr*, custody, property, *talaq*). Each of these conflicts points to the continued cultural and legal dominance of men in regulating the activities of women formulated in terms of the honour code and *Shari'a* law.[12]

Honour Counts

On their way home from working on their landlord's fields in north Lebanon two tenants saw the landlord's unmarried daughter in the orchards in the embrace of a village man. They visited the landlord to report the incident hoping they could use it to bargain with him for higher wages in return for their silence. The landlord replied, 'Look, I can buy virtue for my daughter, you cannot. You had better return home quickly and guard your daughters' virtue well!'

The need to tightly control domestic space is the strategy of the poor, here the Muslim immigrant poor. It is the perception that necessity demands vigilance.[13] Trapped in a social space they can only occupy directly, they subscribe to a view of the world that social order and justice comes from strict moral behaviour, of action in accordance with virtue. Men in this world become the guardians of morality because of their inability to manipulate social reality with other forms of cultural capital.

The relationships between husbands and wives, fathers and daughters, and brothers and sisters are the locus of moral regulation. Yet moral rules have never proven particularly reliable as a means of control in any culture. In the city surveillance and supervision rather than trust becomes the cement of social relations. Individual members are bound to domestic space by paternal as well as communal judgement. Surveillance of the body, or its concealment in enclosed space, is the basis of this moral regulation. But the difficulty encountered enforcing obedience in urban space constantly threatens to dissolve the legitimacy of all social authority and to overwhelm the family.

Narratives on supervision and surveillance are abundant in Muslim immigrant lives. Women, no matter what their age, are unable to act independently of the interests of men in their lives. Womanhood (puberty), marriage, and divorce are the moments at which women can potentially challenge authority. Chronologically, women's lives are marked out by events which lead to an intensification of supervision, only diminishing when they pass child-bearing age.

Education, work and marriage test the extent to which constant supervision will (or can) be a basis for the maintenance of patriarchal authority. Each raises the question of the degree of choice in pursuing different opportunities presented by migration, the possibilities of there being social trajectories of choice.

Domestic confinement is the most extreme response to the challenges to patriarchal authority in migration. Maximum control over gender relations in the household is sought by restricting individual mobility; when outside the household women must observe strict dress codes (*hijab*) in the name of religious morality – and cultural authenticity.

But the strategy of confinement is constructed on difficult premises – that families can afford to live on single wage incomes, that wives can afford to be confined to domestic roles and that daughters can be withdrawn from school when they reach puberty. The political economy of confinement is costly and time consuming for the men who chose it. But the localised basis for cultural reproduction is premised upon the internationalisation of symbolic legitimacy. Strategies conceived in 'honour' are ultimately regulated through Islamic networks and religious authority which relate to a global community and culture.

Disputes over the regulation of unmarried and married women articulate the strategies of surveillance, community interdependence and symbolic production. The surveillance of unmarried women is an issue of paternal authority, the supervision of married women, the authority of husbands over their wives.

Unmarried Women

The socialisation of young women is a central theme in the maintenance of patriarchal authority. The cultural education of women into appropriate sex roles and their obedience to men is reinforced by their socialisation into forms of constraint in the unavoidable public world of the city. Strict supervision of social interaction and close scrutiny of activities outside the household are the most common strategies of regulation for Muslim fathers. The other form of regulation is symbolic control of the body through the maintenance of strict dress codes and the observance of *hijab* (concealment).

The issue of symbolic regulation through veiling arises early because the authority of domestic space is challenged by compulsory schooling and values that invade the house through the mass media, especially television. Paternal authority confronts the reality of class and cultural diversity as well as mass youth culture. From a young age (often from the age of five), much younger than in most parts of the Muslim world, girls are encouraged to wear a scarf. Hijab is strongly advocated in the small number of Islamic schools as a symbol of cultural authenticity and identity in a multicultural society.

Paternal authority confronts the state in the public schools. Insistence on conservative dress codes imposes constraints on all activities which involve exertion or public display of the body. Headscarves are common and accepted. In Australia have never provoked the controversy that famously occurred in French state schools.[14] Muslim fathers frequently object to their daughters participating in any kind of mixed gender sports at school, especially swimming - a major recreational activity in the Australian body beautiful beach culture. The covering required (jeans, shirts or loose smocks) makes participation almost impossible. School accommodation of these practices is made on the grounds of cultural authenticity and sensitivity towards cultural diversity.

The projection of the demands of paternal authority in public space is by no means unique to Muslim immigrants. Many Mediterranean migrants (Greeks, Italians, Yugoslav, Spanish and Egyptian) have pursued similar strategies of surveillance and supervision of their daughters in Sydney. But in these cases honour, especially chastity, is not generally assimilated into a broader cultural identity. Commentary on 'Muslim gender discrimination' is not a statement about 'some fathers' or about class practice. The critique of local immigrant practice is connected to occidental narratives on the nature of Muslim society and Islam and to international cultural politics. Resistance to the construction of patriarchal authority in domestic space is interpreted as evidence that the practice of Islam in the West is a siege activity. Critiques of gender practices are thus received as part of historical narratives about Western imperialism and the cultural degradation of the Other which have a long colonial history.[15]

The critique of gender is strongest in its attack on the alleged practices of clitoridectomy amongst Muslim immigrants. The critique has been taken up in Australia, especially by feminists, as symbolic of the extreme sexual repression of Muslim girls.[16] While very few cases of clitoridectomy have been documented in Australia, the Family Law Council recently specifically recommended legislating against the practice.[17] Politically, the intimacy of the space it challenges, a space of silence as Alice Walker records, is so symbiotically constructed in gender terms that even to speak of it is an act of betrayal.[18] Consequently, the Muslim community response to this kind of allegation is to immediately translate it into evidence of racism and cultural imperialism and a matter for Islamic solidarity. Muslim women's organisations adopt a similar stance declaring such practices are not Islamic and that to suggest otherwise is simply racist, Orientalist.

One resolution to the limits of paternal supervision and surveillance in the multicultural city is marriage, handing over responsibility for one's daughters to husband as soon after puberty as possible. Marriage enables one to order the social world within the certainties of institutional interests. However, the remedy of marriage as a way of protecting honour – being in the right – is circumscribed by Australian state law which prohibits early marriage now 18 years.[19]

Early Marriage

In 1978 a dispute arose between two Shi'i families, the Yousef's and the Hussain's, over a proposal of marriage by Ibrahim Hussein for the hand of Nada Yousef. Ibrahim, the eldest son, was 22 years of age and Nada, the youngest sister, was 14 years. The conflict occurred because Nada's brother, Ahmad, the head of the Yousef household, opposed the marriage. He felt the status of the Hussain family was too low and that his sister should continue her education and pursue a career. Moreover, according to Australian law, Nada was below marriageable age.[20] However, the matter did not end there because of the currency of the Shari'a and of honour in the community. Ahmad could not make decisions which were independent of the scrutiny of the Shi'i community.

Nada came from a well-established Shi'i family in Sydney and lived in an extended household with her eldest brother Ahmad, his working wife and their three children, and her widowed mother. Ahmad was head of the family and an influential leader in the Shi'i community. This extended household was part of a consanguinal group of four married brothers who lived in separate nuclear households close by. They lived amongst other Lebanese Shi'i migrants who had concentrated in this municipality.

Ibrahim was from a recently migrated family and lived about a kilometre away in the same suburb. He was the eldest of five children all of whom lived at home in their father's house. Both families were from the same village in South Lebanon but were unrelated. Nada had met Ibrahim while visiting his two sisters to help them learn English. A friendship had grown between Ibrahim and Nada and led to Abu Ibrahim (Ibrahim Hussain's father) approaching Ahmad Yousef and proposing the marriage of the couple.

Abu Ibrahim saw no obstacles to the marriage. From his perspective the couple wanted to marry and Ibrahim had a job to support Nada. The marriage was also supported by Nada's mother and Nada was old enough to marry under Shari'a law. Abu Ibrahim felt the Australia law was no bar to the marriage because it was religious law and not state civil law that gave legitimacy to marriage in the community.

By mid-1978 the issue of Nada's marriage had become a potentially very serious affair for Ahmad's family and his career. He had become extremely concerned that Nada's public indiscretions, under the surveillance of the Shi'i community, might force him to protect his own standing and his family's honour in the community by imposing strict supervision on her The issue of Ibrahim's family's status was now overshadowed by the consequences of family shame if Nada was accused of sexual intimacy. Hussain and his son Ibrahim understood this and threatened Ahmad that the couple would elope to Lebanon and marry there if he did not change his mind.

Ahmad's choices were to persuade Nada to abandon the proposed marriage, to continue to oppose the marriage and strictly supervise Nada's activities – even, as a last resort, withdraw her from school completely and confine her to the house with her mother, or allow the marriage to go ahead under Shari'a law.

Nada was adamant about the marriage which she saw as allowing her freedom from her brother's supervision, the freedom other non-Lebanese girls at school had. Strict supervision outside the household was difficult because there were so many occasions on which Nada and Ibrahim could meet and be seen in public. There was also the problem of Ibrahim's large Valiant Chrysler which provided great opportunities for sexual intimacy. Withdrawal from school and confinement was also problematic because Nada's mother was in favour of the marriage. The easiest solution was to marry her to Ibrahim by proxy marriage under Shari'a law. But this was not as easy for Ahmad as Hussain suggested. It involved more than a nikkah ceremony with witness and the consent of the proposed bride and groom. The marriage of a girl of 14 under a religious law would be illegal under Australian law.

The illegality of the proposed marriage was of as much concern to Ahmad as protecting the family's honour. Ahmad was an influential Shi'i leader and intermediary with a government job. His prestige in the community and in government and welfare institutions were equally important to his political survival in the Shi'i community.

Disregard for the Australian law could easily be used by political opponents to discredit him and jeopardise his job as an ethnic worker. This could ruin his very successful career as a community leader and intermediary.

Ahmad could not reject the formulation of the dispute in terms of honour because his material and political interests were so closely bound up with the affairs of the community. He had made the community the medium of his political influence. To deny honour would contradict his actions in other areas. Moreover, it would dishonour his adversary Hussain – for all men are not equal in honour and one dishonours oneself if one treats a weaker opponent too heavy handedly. To deny honour would dishonour himself.

Therefore Ahmad's more liberal ideas on his sister Nada's future had to submit to the values the community subscribed to, and to which he had to comply. The question then became which law, Australian or Shari'a, could be used to formalise the agreement reached in honour.

Ahmad sought to save face and preserve his domestic and community standing by introducing the local magistrate into the dispute. In this way he would delay the marriage until Nada became of legal marriageable age, or perhaps even manage to persuade her not to marry. By taking the issue to the local magistrate Ahmad forced Hussain and his son Ibrahim into a court appearance. Short of eloping to Lebanon, Nada and Ibrahim were obliged to wait. Ahmad's experience with the court through his job as an ethnic worker providing cultural information or occasionally acting as an interpreter gave him the upper hand.

The outcome of the interview with the magistrate was to delay the decision for four months when Nada had turned 15 years, the minimum age the magistrate felt he could allow the marriage. In January he would see if circumstances had changed. Ahmad's strategy of going to court had been successful in moving some of the burden of responsibility of the delay in the marriage onto the magistrate's shoulders.

In December, an opportunity for compromise between the two family heads arose with the departure of a visiting Shi'i shaikh. During October and November Ahmad had been lobbying to obtain a resident's visa for a visiting Lebanese Shi'i shaikh to become the 'spiritual leader' of the Sydney Shi'i community. He had been successful in out-manoeuvering another religious association's attempts to have a visiting Kuwaiti shaikh recognised by the Department of Immigration and Ethnic Affairs. At the beginning of December, the newly installed shaikh was about to return to Lebanon for three months to settle his affairs and bring his wife and six children to Sydney. Ahmad reasoned that it was only correct, seeing the shaikh was going to be absent when the couple were hoping to marry, for him to perform a nikkah ceremony before he left.

The marriage ceremony was duly performed in accordance with the practice of delayed cohabitation. The couple then waited until the magistrate granted them permission to marry when Nada turned 15 years.[21] *This second ceremony was performed by a marriage celebrant, who also happened to be a Sunni shaikh servicing the wider Australian Muslim community according to Australian civil law. Afterwards Nada moved to her father-in-law's house.*

In the case where girls are of marriageable age under Australian law, there is no legal conflict. The marriage provisions of the *Shari'a* and Marriage Act are fulfilled in one ceremony. The *Shari'a* is observed to formalise the agreement in the 'official' Islamic code and the Marriage Act complied with as a necessary formality imposed on residents of Australia. In this case, where Nada was not of marriageable age, Ahmad was faced with the problem of formalising the marriage in a legal code not recognised by the Australian law.

The story of Nada points to the interdependence between domestic and community spaces in the formation of patriarchal authority. Surveillance, the public judgement of personal behaviour, is a coercive activity which individuals alone cannot ignore if they want to share social worlds. But the dispute conceived in honour –

the regulation of female sexuality – can only be resolved with reference to the legitimacy of Islamic law, embodied in the person of the shaikh and linked to international Islamic clerical networks. Local community consensus over the nature of marriage and the regulation of sexuality circumscribed action and Lebanese religious authority legitimated the solution.

In reality surveillance has its limitations as a mode of control. The collusion of women in their own sexual subordination and their control through symbolic coercion is more common. The most powerful and the most pervasive symbol of cultural control is the adoption of the veil by adolescent women; teenage schoolgirls often express great satisfaction at being able to wear the veil, while those who do not frequently express their admiration for those who have the courage to do something that sets them apart. Education as an avenue of social mobility is largely new for these working class Muslim families who would not have had the resources or cultural capital to secure higher education in Lebanon. Study by daughters is a double 'coming out', being educated and asserting their individuality, albeit within the constraints of symbolic controls. Some even invert feminist discourse on sexual display to justify their actions in two worlds. They argue that *hijab* is an act of women's empowerment because through concealment they avoid being reduced to sexual objects.

A similar phenomenon occurs amongst Muslim women students from Malaysia and Iran in Australia. The observance of strict dress codes, far removed from the surveillance of their communities and their fathers, is for them an act of good faith in their return as single, chaste and qualified daughters.

Wives

Marriage is central to cultural reproduction and the maintenance of patriarchal authority amongst Muslim immigrants. Arranged marriage, the prioritising of consanguinal over conjugal interests, is reinforced by the Islamic sanction against Muslim women marrying non-Muslim men. In Australia arranged marriage, or more often parent's approval in the selection of marriage, is strongly upheld amongst the first generation. Compared with other Mediterranean immigrant groups, its incidence is considerably higher amongst first and second generation.

The arranging of a marriage occurs across domestic and community space, either a local immigrant community or one in Lebanon. In both the same kinds of social reciprocities are involved and the same cultural referents, family status (*'asl*) and consanguinity, are employed to weigh up the suitability of marriage partners.[22] The focus of these calculations is cultural and social continuity as the basis of security. Social reciprocity is viewed as the product of socialisation within domestic and community space and therefore only capable of reproduction through the correct application of cultural capital. If a marriage into a family in Lebanon secures patriarchal authority, then that is constructive. But knowledge of each other, through genealogy or generational depth, is also the basis for constructing cultural continuity.

Marriages are arranged between families who assemble biographical narratives which remember the history of their good relations. In these marriages, between immigrant families, or between a family in Lebanon and Australia, biography is the basis for creating fictive genealogical ties. These narratives serve to attach the space of immigrant community to another 'place' and all the social and cultural referents it implies.

The strongest expression of continuity through action according to genealogical prescription is parallel cousin marriage. A genealogical model is invoked as the basis of organising social life. But as with all such models, actions in terms of the rules are second order strategies. The observance of parallel-cousin (father's brother's daugther) marriage may be culturally edifying, but it can also be quite pragmatic; a way to fulfil debts incurred in migration, a way to secure the migration of family members who cannot be recruited under the restricted categories of state immigration policy, or a way to enforce patriarchal authority in the consanguinal group despite the subversive impact of immigration.

The incidence of parallel cousin marriages among Muslim immigrants is difficult to determine since it is not officially recorded. Moreover, because there is a cultural (although not legal) taboo against all first cousin marriage in the dominant Australian society, its investigation is difficult. Even imams will often deliberately avoid raising the question when couples come to them to marry because of the taboo against their relationship in the wider society. However, surveys of marriage registers suggest that its practice continues at a rate higher than the cultural norm of around 10 per cent in the Middle East. The strongest indication of its continued practice comes from the childbirth studies of Lebanese-born women in Sydney. Of a sample of 400 Christian and Muslim Lebanese-born women 16 per cent were first cousin marriages and 20 per cent from second or other close blood relatives.[23] The study also found that the first cousin marriage was higher amongst the Muslim women in the sample.

The amount of bridewealth (*al-mahr*) stipulated in an Islamic marriage contract is an expression of consanguinal interest in the marriage. Its size can signify different things, depending on the wealth, poverty or genealogical proximity of the families. In Islamic law bridewealth (*al-mahr*) was designed to ensure the welfare of the wife in the event of divorce or widowhood. Genealogical proximity diminished the amount stipulated because marriage within the consanguinal group was considered much more secure. It represented '... the maximum of integration for the minimal group'.[24] Various Arab proverbs comment on the dangers of marriage to a stranger compared with marriage to kin. One such Lebanese proverb comments: 'A cousin may chew you but he will not eat you!' while a North African proverb observes, 'First madness (daring, risky step): to give the daughter of *'amm* (father's brother) to other men. Second madness: to go penniless to market. Third madness: to vie with the lions of the mountain tops.'[25] By contrast, among wealthy and prestigious families a large bridewealth signifies status rather than genealogical distance.

In migration marriage with reference to genealogy is a measure of necessity and social reciprocity in social life. Genealogical models of parallel cousin marriage have at times been interpreted as a male right – that male cousins should have first chance to marry a cousin over all other comers.

Abduction and Cousin-Right Marriage

Wafa, a fourteen year-old Sunni Muslim girl, was abducted by Walid, a parallel-cousin with the help of his two brothers and two cousins. The reason for the abduction was to insist on his claim to cousin-right in marriage. However, Walid's uncle, Mahmud – Wafa's father – opposed the marriage on two grounds. Firstly, according to custom, the eldest unmarried daughter should marry before her younger sisters (Wafa was the second daughter), and secondly, Wafa already wanted to marry another Lebanese boy and not her cousin. Her father was happy about these plans.

With Wafa's birthday only a month away and her plans becoming more definite, Walid decided to make a last desperate bid to persuade her to change her mind. He intercepted her on her way to work one morning and insisted she come with him to an aunt's place to talk. She reluctantly agreed and was bundled into the back seat of a car with Walid's brothers and cousins who he had brought along for support.

He took her to an aunt's place where they all remained discussing the marriage until early that afternoon. Wafa remained firm about her plans to marry her boyfriend and insisted on telephoning her uncle to come and collect her.

It might have ended there had not been for a newspaper photographer who captured 'the abduction' on camera and emblazoned the pictures on the front page of the afternoon edition of the newspaper. As a result the police arrested and charged the brothers and cousins with abduction.

When the matter eventually got to court the dispute no longer had much significance for the families. The issue of cousin-right was dead and both families closed ranks to downplay the apparent seriousness of the abduction charge. Wafa herself declared that she had not been frightened and thought the incident was just an immature prank. The magistrate dismissed the case and rebuked the cousins for behaving in such a puerile manner.

Marriage shifts the burden of responsibility for a woman from her father to her husband. The main concerns shift from issues of confinement, age of marriage and choice of partner to the sexual division of labour, motherhood and wifely obedience. In Islamic marriage a wife undertakes to be obedient to her husband. A wife who leaves her husband's home without his permission is seen in Islamic law to be rebellious (*nashiza*) and loses her right to maintenance (*nafaqa*). The corresponding duty of the husband is to provide maintenance and to pay the delayed bridewealth (*mu'akhar*).

After marriage confinement is as much a strategy of regulation as it is the consequence of the demands of motherhood and household work. Certainly many Muslim women find their lives enclosed within domestic space. One indication is the very low participation rate of Muslim women in the workforce, another their isolation from medical services during pregnancy and the considerable problems experienced with miscarriage, childbirth and post-natal infant ill health.[26]

In marriage the sexual division of labour is central to the production of material and symbolic culture. Domestic space is the site where family is reproduced, both physically and culturally. Large families make children a significant part of domestic work for women. Cultural knowledge includes Arabic language, religious practice, family history as well as cooking. However, this knowledge is generally 'domestic '. Arabic absorbed in the home, for example, is learned only as a spoken language in an attenuated form, and not as the basis for literate culture.

Food is another important part of cultural knowledge and consumption that is mainly produced at home. It features prominently in Arab culture as the basis of social exchange and creating relations between strangers. As Bourdieu observes, 'The meal is an act of exchange which seals an alliance, which unites strangers in a relationship analogous to kinship.'[27] The production of food often involves growing essential ingredients such as parsley, lettuce, tomatoes, cucumbers, and beans in home gardens – after all the 'best' food comes from the garden – as well as preparing and cooking the food. The commitment to provide daily favourite dishes such as *tabbouli*, *kibbe*, vine leaves, and pastries is time consuming and tiring.

The strong cultural associations with food and nurturing also impose the burden of cooking on mothers. Men certainly cook, they demonstrate this when they put the whole family to work in Lebanese restaurants and help in the kitchen; nevertheless, the domestic production of food has strong maternal associations. Comments such as: 'only my mother knows how to cook'; 'I don't like eating outside'; 'my mother's food is the best' echo the nurturing theme. The strong preference for home-cooked food is a major reason why the Lebanese are not the main patrons of Lebanese restaurants, unlike Chinese and Vietnamese immigrants who patronise ethnic restaurants as community institutions.

The close association of production and consumption of food with sexuality and the intimacy of domestic space is also reflected in the sexual division of labour in making particular foods.

Home Cooking

In 1989 I organised the filming of the preparation of Lebanese food in a Sunni Muslim household for a local multicultural television station. The family, who owned a Lebanese restaurant, prepared a range of dishes including tabbouli (a parsley salad), homos (a chickpea dip), stuffed kibbe (a ground lamb and wheat casing filled with pine nuts, rice and spices) and kafta (ground beef shaped as a sausage) at home for the filming. Three brothers and their wives were involved in the preparation.

Later that evening, after the completion of the filming, the eldest brother rang me to express his concern over the filming of the preparation of the kafta.. He was worried that the camera had been too intrusive in filming close-up the shaping of the kafta by his wife's hands. He asked that this sequence be edited out. His discomfort was over the phallic symbolism in the preparation of the kafta.

Food is an important element of cultural production and identity in migration, strongly influencing the sexual division of labour in domestic space. The necessity of food, its labour input and freshness, is constructed within a daily schedule of readiness, and daily chores are synchronised with the production of food when it is wanted. Readiness to serve one's husband and family is often expanded in migration to include wider hospitality for family and friends. In some cases households from the same family borrow from each other just to be able to maintain an appropriate level of hospitality. In this way, the greater affluence of a household can actually lead to the intensification of food production because of greater demands imposed by a husband's offers of hospitality as a traditional measure of status and a capacity to create social indebtedness.

However, despite preferred cultural practice, the domestic division of labour is governed by need – most husbands cannot afford to withdraw their wives from wage labour to be deployed in the accumulation of other forms of cultural capital. The response to the need for income, and the desire to maintain maximum control over the household, has led to diverse strategies. Some send young children to Lebanon to stay with their grandparents, and even to board in religious institutions, to enable both spouses to work. Alternatively, grandparents are brought to Australia to provide childcare at home while parents work. Others organise the household as an economic unit by entering small businesses, especially restaurants, video shops and petrol stations where they can use family labour without having to disperse profits as wages. Yet others maximise income by pooling wages and redistributing it according to the needs of individual members – getting married, buying property, or education. Large families can often resist economic pressures, even though having many children imposes the logic of domestic confinement – staying at home to care for the family.

Having wives work to provide additional outcome, or become main income earners – increasingly the case in the context of high unemployment among men – makes it difficult to guard domestic boundaries. Where husbands have become long term unemployed through injury, supervision becomes one of the few remaining ways of exercising control in the household. Outside the house the only available forms of regulation are the imposition of cultural symbols of obedience and the use of social surveillance by other family members or friends in the workplace. The headscarf becomes a symbol of a husband's or father's permission to work and the workplace, with family or friends working alongside, becomes a supervised cultural space. There is a cruel irony for veiled Lebanese women in their 'coming out' into employment dressed in a headscarf. At the moment they seek greater independence, or even assume financial responsibility for their families, they experience rejection and discrimination by non-Muslim workers because of their appearance. Employers as a consequence are reluctant to employ workers who may upset the prejudices of the majority of the workforce.

Another form of supervision is to chaperone wives and daughters by car to their work place. By staggering their shift work husbands can also drive their wives or daughters to and from work, thereby avoiding travel in public transport and ensuring maximum supervision of time spent outside the house. At one large biscuit factory in Sydney which employed many Turkish and Lebanese women the immanent change of shift was announced by the arrival of many Turkish and Lebanese husbands in their cars double parked outside the factory gates. Of course there are limits to such close supervision.

A variety of institutions still guard the boundaries of domestic space, especially in situations of serious conflict. They include other kin households, shaikhs and Islamic women's refuges. Traditionally, a wife's first resort in a dispute with her husband was her own family, especially her father. 'Leaving the house in anger' involved introducing one's father (or brother if he was the household head) to mediate in a dispute with one's husband. Whether the dispute was over money, violence, sexuality or the division of labour, but essentially it involved rebellion against a husband's treatment.

Getting Kin Support

Fatima left her husband's (Nazim's) house to stay with her brother after she was beaten and sexually abused by him. Her husband's household was an extended domestic group which consisted of herself, her husband, their 4 year old son, the husband's parents, three unmarried brothers and two unmarried sisters. She had been distressed in their five-year-old marriage because her life was continually interfered with and controlled by Nazim's family, particularly his brothers. She was always bossed around and treated as nothing, even though she had provided a son.

She had gone to her brother's house, the only family she had in Australia except for two uncles. Her brother believed her claims of violence, as did the rest of her family back in Lebanon. In response her husband put it around that she had had an affair with another man and threatened to take revenge for the shame she had brought on him.

The young wife was frightened and desperate and had did not have the confidence to confide in others or seek help, believing that everyone would be against her and insist that she return to her husband and child. Nazim warned her against going to an Australian court, threatening to kill her if she did. He also argued that because theirs was a Shari'a marriage, a dissolution would be governed by the Shari'a.

Her brother and uncles decided she was too difficult to look after in Sydney and suggested she go home to her mother in Tripoli. She planned to take her child with her but her husband refused. Finally she opted to go to her father's house in Lebanon, leaving her son with her husband.

Containment of conflict within kin networks is not always available to families in migration, leading to greater reliance on other mediating institutions to guard the boundaries of domestic space. Community surveillance – judgement in honour – is circumscribed in urban space, limited to areas of concentrated settlement. Seeking the support or intervention of the law, or of the welfare services of the wider society can remove wives from the structures of cultural dependence.

The resort to kin networks in a dispute represents not just the mobilisation of resources but a sharing of responsibility to limit its public impact. Excessive violence in the home, for example, occurs in a context where intervention is anticipated, if not calculated in the response. It is when there is no one to intervene that violence can go beyond what was intended. Culturally, behaviour is conceived as occurring within social contexts in which it is beholden on others to assume responsibility at critical moments. Public displays are often a demonstration of culturally endorsed responses, but in the anticipation that they are restrained by others before further consequences flow.

The consequence of a wife leaving home to seek independence can be socially severe if culturally protective strategies are not observed. Certainly there is little acceptance of the idea that Muslim women can live alone in Australia. But particularly threatening to the guardians of domestic space are the safe houses, 'Women's Refuges', set up to provide havens for harassed and battered wives. For Lebanese Muslim women (Christian ones also) to resort to a women's refuge is regarded as a polluting act by the guardians, one from which it is very difficult to be socially rehabilitated.

An attempt to create a culturally protected and legitimate space for women has been the Islamic Women's Refuge established by the Muslim Women's Association in Sydney. The Refuge was conceived as a culturally neutral space in which marital conflicts could be contained through mediation. Its primary aim is conflict resolution and the preservation of marriage. Yet generally the women refuge workers do not have the social influence to effectively mediate alone; but must call on the prestige of the imam at the mosque.

Mediation seeks to bring parties together before the imam to reach an agreement which is recorded and witnessed by both parties. The imam in this instance acts as a notary (*'adul*), validating and conferring his prestige and authority on the written agreement. When notaries sign a document 'they are adding their stature, their word, as reliable witness to a bond that only takes on implications of truth, of interrelationship, by virtue of having received some form of validation.'[28]

But the formal Islamic legal capacity of the imam to enforce any such agreements in Australia is very limited. In the area of personal law the imam is able to perform a valid Islamic marriage ceremony by the legal power invested in him as an Australian civil marriage celebrant. He has no legal capacity to deal with the issues and procedures of divorce or to enforce pre-marriage contracts under Australian law. Neither Islamic law, nor any other religious law, has any official jurisdiction; its only authority is that conferred on it by the 'Muslim community'.

The imam's authority in the community rests upon his prestige and reputation as a 'spiritual guide' and community leader. His reputation in religious learning and knowledge of Islamic law is the basis of community respect. Imams may claim Islamic judicial authority, but the legal institutions and sanctions to enforce their decisions are elsewhere, not in Australia. While an imam may consult international Islamic networks for legal opinion, on particular matters his authority is essentially dependent on a community morality born out of the urban space of ghettoisation – that is, a public morality enforced by the daily mutual scrutiny of each other's behaviour.[29] Islamic authority in Australia is a product of the cultural attribution of authority carried from lives in Lebanon and the generation community as a domain of consensus and identity in migration.

If the Australian courts become involved in a marital conflict the shaikh, and anyone else who seeks to intervene, can only strive to preserve the marriage within the domain of family. An imam has no legal capacity to decide custody arrangements, to determine property settlements or to issue a judicial separation. The principle site of resistance to 'no fault' Family law with its primary concern, the well-being of the children, is domestic space. With no formal legal power incumbent in the shaikh to enforce Islamic personal status laws, except that conceded to him as a civil marriage celebrant, residual legal power lies in the hands of husbands.

The power derives from the absence of Islamic judicial authority. Husbands can use it by threatening divorce – declaring *talaq* – or by refusing to declare *talaq*.[30] The threat of divorce is exercised in the context of legal uncertainty over jurisdictions and consequences; the refusal to declare Islamic divorce is generally used as a way to punish a wife who has pursued a civil divorce in the Australian courts. Because the Australian judicial system does not recognise other law, there is no proper mechanism to effect religious divorce. Religious law has no independent jurisdiction, and therefore no legal effect, except in the communities which observe it. A shaikh can only persuade a husband to declare a divorce and without a religious divorce a wife remains married in the eyes of the community and unable to remarry within that community.

The residual authority of husbands can lead them to manipulate the regulation of domestic space by moving between legal jurisdictions in Australia and Lebanon.

Travel Plans

Mahmud, a Sunni Muslim from Tripoli, was in dispute with his wife and decided he would divorce her. Instead of declaring his intentions to her he decided his best strategy was to return to Lebanon with the whole family to avoid Australian legal jurisdiction which would be less favourable to his interests. He told the family they were returning to Lebanon to live, proceeded to sell the family home and remigrate with all the family. Shortly after arriving in Lebanon he divorced his shocked wife. She not only lost any share in the property they had owned in Australia, but also the custody of her children. Under the Shari'a the money he earned from his employment was his and the custody of children was awarded to him because his sons were older than 7 years and his daughter older than 9 years. By moving back to Lebanon the husband had managed to ensure that the jurisdiction of Shari'a would obtain.

Husbands do not, however, need to return to Lebanon to have the *Shari'a* prevail in their domestic space. The shaikh is the guardian of *Shari'a* law in the immigrant community. He speaks not only as a religious functionary but as a community leader, one who represents collective interests in a multicultural context and guards the moral order of the immigrant community. Although he has no official legal authority in the eyes of the state, his opinions and mediation are backed by his religious learning, credentials and piety and by his political stature as an ethnic leader. Solidarity with the shaikh is a matter of ethnic community pride as well as loyalty; hence to be seen to publicly criticise or oppose him is to shame the community.

The shaikh embodies the political and cultural duality of immigrant community space. His institutional and social status render him a transnational and transcultural agent linking cultural and legal worlds in Lebanon and Australia. As a transcultural agent, his role is to interpret Islamic practice for proletarian Muslim immigrants in a multicultural society. As a legal actor he is the upholder of Islamic law and traditions in the Sunni immigrant community. In this role his formal legal capacities include those of a religio-legal functionary whose actions with respect to Islamic personal status law are recognised by the Islamic Courts in Lebanon, and a civil marriage celebrant appointed by the Australian federal attorney general. However, his 'proxy' legal authority, derived from the Shari'a court in Lebanon, and his communally-based prestige create a Muslim legal and moral environment which lies in a complex interplay of the formation of ethnic identity, social solidarity and cultural maintenance.

When an imam addresses personal law questions based on his proxy Islamic jurisdiction, his position of religious authority is always tested because the legal sanctions he can bring to bear are enforceable elsewhere, not in Australia. Consequently he is forced into a mediating role with his religious standing and community opinion as his principle sanctions. In the context of multicultural politics there have been unsuccessful efforts to make Islamic personal status law valid law for Muslims in Australia.[31] Only in the area of pre-marriage contracts has there been innovation which would allow the enforcement of bridewealth agreements (*al mahr*) through the courts. Prior to this shaikhs had sought to use the sanctions of the Australian court to enforce deferred bridewealth payments through a promissory note signed by the husband to the wife in the event of divorce. In most cases the amount of bridewealth is small

– less than $10,000 – in comparison to the benefits provided by the state in the form of single parent benefits, child allowance and public housing for the most needy. The legal enforcement of delayed bridewealth payments was taken up by the Australian Federation of Islamic Councils in the national review of 'Multiculturalism and the Law' as a issue of gender equity.[32]

One of the common ways the shaikh acts as a transnational legal agent is when he marries people by proxy. In the sequence of 'offer and acceptance' in Islamic marriage, a shaikh can witness the marriage of a person resident in Lebanon through a guardian. The practice of using a marriage guardian (*wilaya al-jibar*) continues in Lebanon almost exclusively in contracting emigrant marriages. The traditional capacity of the guardian being able to contract marriages of a minor without her consent does not apply in Lebanon. These proxy marriages are then recognised as valid by the Australian Government, provided they fulfil the requirements of the Marriage Act.

The shaikh therefore continues to function in a religio-legal capacity, representing the Shari'a Court with all the tangled implications of individuals seeking to attract its jurisdiction from Australia. In addition the right of Lebanese to hold dual nationality facilitates Lebanese mobility between the two legal domains.

Keeping the Courts out of the Home

Once a dispute goes beyond the family it becomes a public matter which comes to the attention of the community, the courts or both. Failure to contain a dispute within the family introduces more influential and powerful individuals who represent the disputants as third parties. Usually no-one wants to make a dispute public because it is always potentially more damaging. It creates debts of future reciprocity or requires costly contributions to mediators. It is also very threatening to reputations and status – to honour.

While Lebanese Muslims are conversant with the prescriptive rules of *Shari'a* law on marriage and divorce, they are still largely ignorant of Australian family law. They are aware of the consequences of court intervention, but not the procedures or philosophy of the law. For them it is an encounter with the state which is unmediated and threatening. Their response is to try to gain some control over the legal process. They shop around, eliciting stories of the court experiences of other Lebanese and getting the legal advice of 'ethnic' solicitors recommended to them by family, friends or acquaintances. They often approach solicitors, not to simply ask advice, but to bargain with them armed with stories about similar disputes and outcomes and what they in turn expect.

Ethnic solicitors are usually second or third generation Lebanese with a knowledge of at least some Arabic and Lebanese culture. Frequently their clientele is built up through community networks. Reputation is everything. Yet in reality they service the needs of an immigrant working class heavily dependent on legal aid to conduct their cases. Divorce, road accidents, workers injury compensation and real estate contracts are their bread and butter.

People often deliberately expand disputes into the community or court arenas as a second order strategy – an attempt to transmute private interests into the disinterested, collective and publicly legitimate. The community and the courts are drawn into a dispute as resources and frameworks in which to structure the discourse of a dispute and determine its outcome. Their involvement may be accepted or rejected by one or both of the disputants. But the expansion of the dispute does not necessarily mean that other arenas are eclipsed. The discourse and procedural modes associated with family, community and the courts often continue in parallel.

The formulation of disputes in terms of honour, *Shari'a* or Australian family law invokes different procedural and settlement modes. Each formulation has its own generative system of rules and resources which define the limits of action and the exercise of power in the family, community and court arenas. The expansion of a dispute usually changes the issues and meaning of the conflict. A conflict over modesty and obedience in the family can become a matter of seclusion or marriage to protect the family's honour in the community. In the courts it may turn into a matter of domestic violence or the eligibility of a minor to marry. But in this system of competitive arenas the ultimate jurisdiction rests with the Australian courts and law.

Domestic Violence

A young Muslim wife who was regularly beaten by her husband eventually went to the police to report a particularly brutal assault by her husband. She was taken to the police station by her father to whose house she had gone, after the beating. The father had tried many times to mediate between his daughter and son-in-law but without success. By going to the police he made the dispute a matter of criminal assault.

However at the last minute the case was withdrawn from court because the wife refused to go ahead with her testimony. She felt intimidated by the husband and feared losing her young son through abduction. She feared her husband would simply take him away to Lebanon at a later date. Despite the assurances of the prosecution that the husband could be legally prevented from doing so she felt that ultimately she had no protection against her husband if he was alienated by a court decision granting her custody. From her point of view the criminal charges had served the purpose of alleviating the assaults. She decided to remain in the marriage and hope for the best.

Once the courts are introduced into a dispute they will always arrive at a legal decision. The sanctions available to them can restrict the strategies simultaneously employed in the family and in community arenas. The court can restrict travel, regulate access to a wife and children, issue temporary custody orders, prevent the removal of the children from Australia, prevent withdrawals from savings accounts and freeze the sale of property or of business assets.

The courts also largely ignore cultural definitions of a conflict in arriving at their decisions. A man who wishes to divorce his wife must comply with the provisions of the Family Law Act; *talaq* divorce has no legal effect, except in community practice. The courts give no recognition to other cultural and legal concepts. Only occasionally are such concepts considered as background to a dispute and shaikhs are rarely, if ever, consulted by a court or its officials.

The *Shari'a* and Australian family law hardly ever confront each other directly in the courts. This only occurs when one party has attempted to avoid the jurisdiction of the Australian courts by obtaining a decision in the Shari'a court in Lebanon. The most common situation is where a wife challenges the Shari'a court's validity under Australian law in order to secure more favourable custody or property arrangements.

Confused Jurisdictions

In a contested divorce a Family Court judge noted that the failure of a husband to lodge any tax returns made it impossible to determine the value of his assets. All he could do was to refer the matter to the Commissioner for Taxation for further investigation.

To the judge's amazement the question of the custody of the children had virtually been left unmentioned. The husband and wife had already agreed to allow the paternal grandparents to care for the children in Lebanon in accordance with Shari'a preference for patrilineal custody. The judge only granted the decree of dissolution after he was satisfied through correspondence with the Lebanese Shari'a court that proper arrangements had been made for the welfare of the children.

In fact the only reason the dispute came to the Family Court was the wife's interest in gaining a share of the husband's assets in Australia.

In terms of the actual outcome of a dispute, however, the courts only limit the jurisdiction of religious law; they do not exclude it. The Australian courts may impose a particular property and custody settlement, but the substance of the settlement may be largely governed by expectations shaped by the *Shari'a*. Hence a husband can secure a desired outcome by using the sanction of withholding a *talaq* divorce, or a couple may present the dissolution of marriage to the Family court as uncontested. Consequently contested positions formulated in terms of subordinate codes (honour and *Shari'a*) persist in a continuing dialogue with each other throughout the course of a dispute in the community or court arenas. The persistence of subordinate codes is the basis of the continuing contest to organise and regulate family relations, to control domestic space; it does not merely represent a preference for procedural modes (e.g. meditation) or Islamic religious and cultural values. The clash is over the family as a traditional support institution and the intervention of the state in guaranteeing the welfare and security of individuals in the face of accelerated family breakdown in the wider Australian society.

What is actualised in a court decision is the product of complex interactions in which subordinate codes seek to limit the impact of the dominant legal system in the regulation of domestic space. But *Shari'a*, patrilineal kinship and honour can only be indirectly articulated in a legal case. In the community, however, the situation is reversed. The dominant legal system represents a structure within which subordinate codes learn to operate. They must accommodate the dominant legal system which in turn alters their very procedures and forms.

Honour and *Shari'a*, unlike Australian family law, are not the sole property of professional legal specialists. In the Australian migration context these codes exist in a dominant cultural and social milieu, which grants them no authority and which shapes and limits their legitimacy and application. The question of what is regular social practice and the cultural norm is uncertain and constantly being tested.

For the Family Court, the 'traditional' values which espouse the moral integrity of the family, marriage obligations and fault divorce have largely been put aside in preference for law which reflects the needs of modern marriage, that is the welfare and security of individual children and dependent wives.

Family Court decisions reflect these changes in attitude towards marriage and divorce and their philosophy of individualism and cultural universalism. The championing of the child's rights, deciding custody on the basis of the environment which would provide the best opportunity for the social development of the child, and underwriting the economic security of individuals through government pensions and benefits are examples of this change.

5

Community and Identity in the City

The symbiosis of family and community, of domestic and communal space in migration is an expression of the way cultural production is built from the bottom up. Individual lives are not regulated by enclosing institutional orders but by the dictates of the social spaces allocated to them. Community is a description of a kind of social space rather than some romantic enactment of gemeinschaft, village solidarity rediscovered in the foreign industrial city. It is the nexus of shared experience, knowledge and place but, while constructed as a domain of autonomy, it is such only ideologically. The appropriation of urban space through interdependent personalised worlds is entrapment within certain social and political possibilities. It is a class location which indicates a limited command of space and symbolic resources.

The city is constituted by a multiplicity of community spaces, distinct social worlds which coexist and overlap and are as much a product of tolerance as their dispersal and social distance in vast urban geographies. People in large cities travel along metaphorical freeways which connect known spaces and allow them to largely ignore what lies between. They jump over social diversity through the privatisation of social life, through the car, the telephone and suburban domesticity:

> Practices and experiences within these spaces provide the grist for consciousness formation. Forbidden spaces, feared spaces, ignored spaces, redundant spaces contain the materials of our own ignorance in the same way as shared spaces, comfortable and challenging spaces, needed spaces, become the proving ground for defining who or what we are.[1]

The city, unlike the construct of the 'imagined community' of nation, is not the site of the homogenisation of social consciousness but its differentiation and, increasingly, internationalisation at all social levels.

Community is constructed out of domestic life, neighbourhood encounters, participation in village association activities and attendance at the mosque, reading the Arabic press and listening to the 'ethnic' radio in Arabic – the recognition of shared experience of social space through the circumscribing medium of Arabic. But this knowledge is not simply about one's own 'community' – some entity transported and reassembled in migration – but knowledge of the wider society, its acceptances, hostilities and denials. What happens when one prays in public (not community) space, tries to find a job, wears a headscarf, plans to build a mosque, wants to observe religious holidays during the working week, or expresses pro-Arab or Muslim views in mixed company.

The urbanisation of 'immigrant consciousness' involves a dialogue between the inside and outside, drawing boundaries around social spaces to assert an autonomy which is very fragile. One of the codes deployed to generate community is honour, judgement about patriarchal performance.[2] It connects men through surveillance of their public acts and supervision of their women. It is in this domain that the official codes – Islamic law – are invoked to legitimate practices.

The community of immigrants relates to particular spaces rather than to a discrete entity. Amongst the Muslim immigrant communities in Australia, as well as Western Europe, the defining social spaces are local and include mosques, village associations and neighbourhoods.[3] These are the sites where groups which are economically and culturally marginal construct 'community' and identity. But they are not circumscribed by local face-to-face relations. Community spaces include the transnational spaces of other diasporas, community of origin, as well as networks generated through membership in political parties or unions.[4] The reference to 'community' in immigration is usually a construct of 'representation', the claim to speak for a collectivity vis-à-vis other sections of the community or wider multicultural society. In fact the diversity of 'community' connects Lebanese with very different social trajectories; the second generation who have gained education and perhaps professional qualifications with the needs and practices of unqualified non-English speakers who have just arrived. But these inhabit the same 'community' only in a limited sense where their life choices and resources intersect. The image of community as culturally homogeneous is as much a construction of the dominant society – the homogenised 'ethnic community' is derivative of the very idea of the nation itself – as of the immigrants themselves. The maps are overlapping rather than a matching overlay.

The everyday reciprocities which map community life are the social life of the street, telephoning family and friends, visiting, shopping, collecting children from school. The appropriation of space (close residence) creates the possibility of the regeneration of subsistence communities. A specific knowledge emerges about where and when you can find people – the coffee shop, playing cards, collecting unemployment benefits, at the mosque – as well as where cheap or illicit goods are available – the fish vendor who sells illegally out of the boot of his car or even where illicit drugs can be bought – or where you might pick up casual work in the black economy, or who is best informed about welfare benefits. The location of businesses selling culturally desirable consumer items such as *halal* meat, Turkish coffee, freshly roasted nuts, a traditional bakery and a pastry shop reinforces and signifies the presence of such informal cultural worlds.

Participation in village associations and other organisations is the formal side of community reciprocity. These focus on mutual aid and serve to socially demarcate collectivities. The celebration of the village is a reaffirmation of the continued significance of place-bound identities among immigrants. Place, family and sect continue to be socially defining and revealing. Panoramic photos of the village displayed at home are visual summaries of this identity and attachment.

Village organisations become the primary forums in which reputation and success are displayed in culturally familiar ways – through leadership, gifts and public speaking. This world of men creates a space in which public performance is an act of integration into an hierarchically conceived social order based on biographies. All men are equal in honour and must participate if they are to be recognised.

But not all men choose to participate. The contraction of socially trusted individuals to immediate kin, through the dislocation of migration, but also the lingering memories of civil war, sees a celebration of the singular integrity of the family – domestic space as refuge and moral self-sufficiency. Immigration provides opportunities to withdraw into family autonomy and avoid community relations which are always potentially debt creating. As one Sunni father expressed it, 'our family has integrity and we do not need to go to the mosque to prove it, anyway, they are too interested in politics there.'

During the civil war (1976–90) period relations between Lebanese immigrant village associations were honed by the ebb and flow of sectarian and regional relations back home. Much of the undercurrent of immigrant life is a constant narrative about the present and its ties to events, biographies and memories in Lebanon. Overall, community space was saturated with the markers of place-bound loyalties, family status and sectarian identity. On the few occasions when this led to serious violence the limits of community autonomy through surveillance – social coercion – were revealed in the intervention of the state, the police and law courts. Even though the conflict could not be contained within the community the legal process did not eclipse the community's role in assessing social responsibility and justice.

Murder and Revenge

Fuad and Khalil had both emigrated from north Lebanon, the former from Tripoli and the latter from a village in Akkar. Fuad had left Tripoli in the early seventies while Khalil had migrated as part of the 'refugee' group after the first stage of the civil war in 1976. Fuad, a Sunni Muslim, was aged 36 and lived with his wife and three young children. Apart from his own household, he had few relatives in Australia except for a paternal cousin, Usman. By contrast Khalil was Maronite Catholic, only 22 years old, unmarried and the eldest son. His household included his parents, an uncle, and his four brothers and sisters who were unmarried. The two men were workmates, lived in the same suburb a few blocks from each other, and occasionally met when visiting mutual friends. They were acquaintances, not good friends.

One evening in 1978 while visiting mutual friends, the Salim brothers, they argued with each other. The background to the argument was the politics of the civil war and the issue of political commitment to causes. Fuad was from a traditional Sunni Arab nationalist family while Khalil was from a family who were recruited as strong-arm men for the local Christian political figures. According to the Salim brothers Fuad and Khalil got into an argument about the servile character of the people of Akkar, Khalil's home district. Fuad had asserted that it was common knowledge that people from Akkar readily followed leaders. Khalil took offence at the comment and stormed out of the house angry at the insult against the people of Akkar.

Later the same evening Khalil, with his uncle, lay in wait for Fuad as he walked home. When Fuad reached them Khalil and his uncle beat him with sticks and left. There were no other witnesses to the attack. The Salim brothers learned about the beating the same evening when Khalil's younger brother, under instruction from his father, arrived at their home with a request that they act as intermediaries between Khalil and Fuad. The younger brother reported that Khalil had beaten up Fuad for his insult and that the father wanted to prevent further revenge attacks. The Salim brothers angrily declined.

Khalil's father's fears proved to be well founded. The following day Fuad and Khalil became involved in a street brawl outside the factory where they both worked. Fuad waited for Khalil at the beginning of the afternoon shift and attacked Khalil with a lump of wood. During the fight Khalil had drawn a knife and stabbed Fuad, causing a fatal wound. Khalil fled in his car but was arrested soon after at the scene of a car accident in a neighbouring suburb and charged with murder.

The dispute which began with an insult over manly honour was escalated by the resort to physical violence resulting in the death of Fuad and the intervention of the police and courts. First Khalil and then Fuad resorted to violence because they felt dishonoured by the other. Khalil felt shamed by the comment about the servility of Akkar men and had responded by seeking his revenge by beating up Fuad. Fuad, in turn, had been outraged and insulted by Khalil's cowardly and excessive attack over what he considered a trivial matter and had retaliated the next day by publicly beating him with a stick.

From the moment of Khalil's arrest the police investigation and community evaluation of responsibility and justice became intertwined. At the committal proceedings Khalil was remanded in custody with bail refused for fear that he would either flee the country or would be the target of a revenge attack. Strong community feeling and the threat, real or imagined, of a 'self-help' remedy immediately shaped the case. Community evaluation of the events focused on the circumstances of both attacks, the responses of significant kin to the death, and the reputations of the men involved. The consensus about these elements emerged during the course of the police investigations and ensuing trial. The mosque association and village association were the principle arenas where information about the details of the attack, developments in the case and the progress of the court hearings were exchanged and discussed. Khalil's family by contrast were quite isolated within the household and a small village community network.

In the mosque community the night attack by Khalil was seen as much more provocative than Fuad's daylight retaliation in front of the factory. While the former was secretive, unseen (at night) and with help the latter was public (in the full light of day), alone, and witnessed by many people at a change of shift. Khalil's attack was seen as a hotheaded reaction while Fuad's retaliation was seen as a justified response aimed at administering a public beating – teaching a lesson – to the younger man to redeem honour.

During the course of the investigations and subsequent trial the behaviour and observations of Khalil's kin to the events were also seen as incriminating. Firstly the attempt by Khalil's father to initiate mediation soon after the night attack on Fuad was interpreted as an acknowledgment of Khalil's responsibility and the potential revenge attack. Secondly, the flight of Khalil's uncle to Lebanon strongly suggested his own involvement in the night beating. In the eyes of the community his flight confirmed his complicity and indicated that he himself feared that he would be the primary target for a revenge attack, given Khalil himself was detained in gaol. The advice Khalil had allegedly given his father, according to witnesses at the scene of the car accident, for him and his brothers to leave Sydney to avoid the threat of retaliation was also seen as incriminating.

The opinion of Khalil's mother about the events was also put forward as damning evidence against Khalil. During the course of the subsequent trial Khalil's mother, in a chance meeting with Fuad's aunt at a shopping mall, had expressed strong disapproval of Khalil's actions saying that he had been very bad to kill a father with three children. Finally Khalil's kin were believed to have prejudiced the outcome of the case by intimidating one of the main witnesses for the prosecution case. The witness, a Greek employee at the factory who had made a statement about the circumstances of the stabbing sold his house and returned permanently to Greece shortly after the committal proceedings in the Coroner's Court.

The reputation of the two men and their social circumstances weighed heavily against Khalil in the community's eyes. While Fuad was a family man with three children Khalil was single without these social obligations – obligations which are culturally considered to constrain behaviour which would unfairly harm others. In short the young man was seen as being irresponsible, while the married man was seen as acting within the context of honour, showing measured force, which would not lead to death or see him charged with a serious crime thereby harming his family.

The image of Khalil as a young hothead fitted the stereotype that Tripoli people had of people from Akkar. In fact it was the issue of the stereotype that had been the trigger for the fight. Khalil, by his violent actions, had fulfilled the stereotype. There were several other stories about Khalil drawing a knife on people in Sydney as a result of arguments which reinforced this view.[5] *Moreover there were rumours that his family had been strong men (qabadayat) for the Kata'ib during the Lebanese civil war and that Khalil himself was responsible for the death of six people.*

The community judged Khalil responsible and anticipated revenge by Fuad's family. The only person able to exact revenge was Usman, Fuad's closest male consanguine living in Sydney however he was unwilling to do so. Firstly, Usman was a well known intermediary in the Sunni community and a revenge killing would not only jeopardise his livelihood and career as well as the future of his wife and children. He reasoned that he would undoubtedly be caught and imprisoned if he pursued a revenge killing in Australia. Secondly, after his cousin's death, he had become the principal police contact and intermediary with the community to marshal information and evidence for the prosecution case. Thirdly, as Khalil had been arrested and detained in gaol very soon after the homicide the opportunity for immediate revenge was denied him.

Usman, nevertheless, still felt he needed to defend his honour. He pursued his personal revenge by assisting the prosecution case with information to ensure Khalil's conviction for murder. He helped police to find witnesses and obtain information about Khalil's reputation and culturally incriminating behaviour of both Khalil and his family. Usman sought to present a story which, in the community's eyes, would be damning of Khalil and persuasive to the court. He pointed out that a man does not act alone in such a serious crime but with the support and backing of his family. To act alone is the mark of a stupid man.[6]

At the same time he did not publicly renounce revenge. He advised police that the threat of violence to Khalil's family was serious enough to warrant placing a police guard on the family's house. No attack eventuated occurred but the fact that the police visited Khalil's family to warn them about the threats against them were demeaning– as if to say, 'Even the police take our threats seriously, so must you!' During the court proceedings Usman had even toyed with the idea of rushing down to the accused and punching him in a public display of rage just to avenge his honour.[7]

In brief, community opinion was that Khalil had a reputation for being hot-tempered, aggressive, too ready to use a knife, and had intentionally killed a married man who had a young family. Fuad, the deceased, had only attacked Khalil after extreme provocation and had only intended to give Khalil a good beating, something it was generally agreed he deserved.

Yet, while persuasive in the community this assessment proved worthless in the court because it either lacked sufficient detail and proof or was ruled irrelevant to the circumstances surrounding the attack. Actions the community saw as damning were eliminated by strict rules of legal evidence. Legally the issue amounted to whether Khalil's action in drawing a knife was merely an act of self-defence by a smaller man under attack by a larger man with a lump of wood, and hence did not constitute excessive use of force in self-defence. Khalil was not the aggressor in this instance but did he deliberately come back to stab the deceased after numerous people had separated them and restrained his attacker?

Khalil was acquitted and the community felt cheated of justice. They blamed the quality of the prosecution which they believed to be inferior to that of the defence – after all they could buy the best legal expertise available while the aggrieved parties had to accept a government prosecutor. The jury, consisting of ordinary people with no special status or legal and cultural knowledge, were regarded as inadequate to the task of making such an important decision. Moreover, the presence of a well-known Lebanese legal tout (a person who gets business in the Lebanese community for a firm of solicitors) and the convenient disappearance of a principal prosecution witness, all suggested to the interference in the judicial process.

Khalil, for his part, knew that on his release he had no option but to leave Sydney and his family because of strong community opinion against him and the possible threat of revenge. Thus while he had won the court case this was at considerable financial cost to his family and he suffered the social humiliation of expulsion from the Sydney communities.

Khalil's murder and the community response to it revealed the currency of honour and closeness of the immigrant community in urban space. Information about the circumstances of events, reputations and kin responses forged community opinion in the social context of associational life. While information about the past in Lebanon was relevant, the immigrant context and community were the primary arena.

The nexus between community and practice is not always so parochial, it can be transnational. The flux of alliances and fortunes of civil war in Lebanon often led to considerable confusion in community relations in Sydney. The idea of community as 'representation' was particularly evident in this context. Associations were constituted through reciprocity (mutual aid, sociality) and status competition. Ambition for leadership of an association was an opportunity to 'speak for' others. This claim to 'represent' others occurred in the context of other Lebanese associations, but also vis-à-vis the broader multicultural society where one could claim the role of intermediary or cultural broker on the grounds of special knowledge of the nuances of difference in the Lebanese communities. The claim to 'represent' others was built upon place and identity – village, region and sect. At the broadest level there were claims to leadership of the 'Lebanese community' (across generations and sect). However, these were highly contentious and usually served to emphasise sectarian differences.

The state's role in confirming the mantle of spokesperson/leadership through visits and grants was to underwrite the social reciprocity and difference that the occupation of urban space imposed upon them. To claim special knowledge of the networks, biographies and needs of a single village community was to confirm the social basis of reconstituting identity within the logic of the urban process.

But the undercurrent of the war tended to produce situations in which groups who were friends and allies on one day suddenly found themselves enemies the next, even though nothing in Sydney had changed to influence the relations in communities. The nexus of identity in Sydney and Lebanon clashed and produced unpredictable politics, constantly rearranging relations between immigrant associations. This had the effect of making community the focus of mobilisation, but also an attachment which often proved to be volatile.

Political organisations were especially responsive to the climate of the civil war. While they were distinct from village associations they were not completely detached. Most supra-village organisations were in fact built upon village communities. Village associations were the focus for recruitment into broader political organisations and office in a village association was used as a springboard to realise aspirations in political organisations. Consequently a falling out in Lebanon between parties or groups had repercussions in the political and overlapping village organisations in Sydney.

Intense competition among men for status in the context of community resulted in a proliferation of associations and led to the establishment of branches of most Lebanese political parties in Sydney, often very small ones. Political aspirants amongst Lebanese immigrants would communicate with parties in Lebanon and offer to establish a branch in Sydney. Sometimes the parties recruited broadly, as in the case of the Syrian Socialist Nationalist Party, Kata'ib, and Amal, and sometimes very narrowly as in the case of the Lebanese Communist Party or the Iraqi Ba'th Party. On occasions branch membership amounted to little more than the members of an extended family.

Conflict between Lebanese party branches generally took the form of attacks on the reputations of political and religious community leaders. Conducted in the Arabic press, radio programmes, through graffiti, and in sermons in the mosques and churches, these campaigns were not contained within the communities but extended into the Australian political arena by various mechanisms. Firstly, government agencies maintained daily casual surveillance over the ethnic press and radio. Hence Arabic editorials would be noticed by parts of the bureaucracy charged with looking after the needs of, and keeping an eye on, ethnic communities. Lebanese community leaders used the media to register their opinions and conduct their campaigns against opponents. Even the mainstream Australian press was at the time inadvertently drawn into 'Lebanese stories' and political campaigns through the use of networks.

In the most intense conflicts, Australian politicians, government agencies, the media and the courts all became resources to marshal support against opponents, to have them discredited and, if possible, deported under provisions of the immigration law. Long campaigns over several years were conducted against Aboud, head of the SSNP in Australia, and Shaikh Tajuddin al-Hilaly, the Imam at the Sunni Lebanese mosque and former leading member of Tawhid, a Sunni Islamist movement in Tripoli. Such campaigns served to focus activities and give a sharp edge to Lebanese immigrant politics.

Fighting Lebanese Political Battles in Sydney

In August 1981, an appeal was heard in the Federal Court of Australia against the deportation of Aboud (Haj-Ismail) made by the minister for immigration and ethnic affairs.[8] The judge found against the minister on the grounds that Aboud had not yet completed the purpose for which he had been originally granted a temporary resident's visa, i.e. to complete a Ph.D., and that he had a 'legitimate expectation' to be allowed to remain until he had completed it. The costs were awarded against the minister.

Aboud had arrived in Australia in 1972 to act as a political organiser for the SSNP, the Syrian Socialist Nationalist Party, a Syrian nationalist party whose headquarters are in Beirut.[9] His task was to form a party branch from the Lebanese communities in Sydney cutting across sectarian cleavages. In order to gain a temporary resident's visa he enrolled as a Ph.D. candidate in political science at a local university. He cut a curious figure at an Australian university often accompanied by a bodyguard.

Under his leadership the SSNP grew to become the largest Arab political association in Sydney, claiming a membership of over 1600 by 1985. The party's strong anti-sectarian ideology was popular, as was its promotion of Arabic culture and language. It held regular community meetings, had its own party newspaper published in Arabic, (an-Nahda, The Renaissance) and built a large and luxuriously appointed social club. However as an organisation it was very hierarchical and regimented.

The popularity of the SSNP concerned other Lebanese associations on both the left and the right of the political spectrum. It was regularly accused of using strong arm tactics against rival associations and Arabic newspapers. In the community its leader made a point of holding provocative meetings to recruit political converts in suburbs which sectarian based Lebanese parties regarded as their province. Hence the SSNP came into conflict with the Kata'ib in Maronite suburbs, Hizbollah in Shi'i suburbs and the Murabitoun in Sunni suburbs. On one occasion this led to a street brawl between around 150 people from the SSNP and a rival political group. On another occasion the editor of a rival Arabic newspaper who had criticised the SSNP in an editorial was beaten up, allegedly by members of that association.[10]

In order to counter the SSNP's growing following, leaders of several rival associations lobbied Australian politicians and bureaucrats to have Aboud's application to renew his visa rejected. After Commonwealth police investigations into the party – slightly delayed by a romantic affair between a senior officer and a prominent woman party activist – the minister for immigration and ethnic affairs granted permanent resident status. He concluded from the investigations that Aboud failed to meet the requirements of 'good character' and ordered that he be deported.

Aboud organised a skilful legal defence and public campaign to be allowed to remain in the country. Firstly, he took defamation actions against several Arabic newspapers in Sydney and argued that deportation would prejudice his chances. Secondly, a Committee for the Defence of Aboud was organised amongst party members and 5,000 signatures were collected in a public campaign affirming his 'good character' and supporting his application for permanent resident status. Thirdly, proceedings were instituted in the Federal Court against his deportation. His appeal against the minister's deportation order was successful.

The recreation of a Lebanese political world through the mobilisation of place, family and sect identity was linked to the broader process of integration into Australian multicultural society. The confusions over identity and allegiance projected from the Lebanese civil war could be subordinated to the question of identity in the larger Australian society. Intra-Lebanese conflicts actually helped define the boundaries of community and the specificity of sect in the Australian context. Hence the socialisation of Lebanese into Lebanese Muslim or Lebanese Christian communities defined competitive relations vis-à-vis the larger construction of Australian cultural pluralism. These identities articulated not only cultural specificity and community boundaries but also their cultural desirability measured in terms of their 'success' – social mobility.

While political disputes between associations informed the Lebanese about cleavages and the relevance of place, family and sect in urban space, it was conflicts over religious practice and leadership which became the focus for defining their relations with the broader Australian society.

Rivalry over sect focused on the changed demography of Lebanese immigrants as a result of the arrival of refugees. The ethnic voice of the Lebanese changed from an overwhelmingly Christian Maronite and Orthodox one to one which reflected more closely the religious diversity of Lebanon. The strong assertion of sectarian identity in Sydney so shocked one Maronite priest who had served for a long time in northern Argentina – he felt the worst of Lebanese politics had been recreated in Sydney – that he eventually returned to Argentina to escape it. In Argentina, where immigration had ceased decades earlier, generational distance from Lebanon and cultural homogeneity had made sect a source of solidarity rather than demarcation of distance.

The Shaikh as Ethnic Leader

Religious leadership in the Sunni and Shi'i communities emerged out of the ritual and spiritual needs of Muslim immigrants. The locally grown nature of Muslim religious organisation and culture was characteristic of most immigrant minority religions in Australia. However, because of the absence of a 'church' in Islam the Muslim immigrants did not experience the institutionalisation of religious life by the subsequent immigration of 'ethnic' churches. For most Mediterranean migrants religious life was initially organised around the needs of families and village communities and only subsequently institutionally incorporated, sometimes willingly and sometimes not, into their own ethnic churches.[11] *The religious life of the Lebanese Maronite and Orthodox communities followed this pattern. By contrast, Islamic organisation remained the product of the efforts of local communities from diverse cultural and linguistic backgrounds.*

The establishment of mosques and the recruitment of clerical leadership grew out of associational politics – out of the appropriation of local urban space as Muslim. In the early 1960s religious activities in the Lebanese Sunni community crystallised around the activities of a devout Sunni Muslim from Tripoli, Khalil Chami. He assumed the position of shaikh through community recognition of his piety, welfare work and religious learning, even though he had undertaken no formal religious training. His success was built upon his personal charisma and his tireless and self-sacrificing efforts to assist anyone who asked for his help. His religious standing was further enhanced by his official appointment as an Australian civil marriage celebrant which enabled him to perform religious marriages valid under Australian law. He organised the use of a house for prayer and was heavily involved in planning a new mosque to be built on the same site. In addition he published a monthly religious magazine in Arabic which focused on Islamic religious matters in Australia and the Middle East.

In the 1970s the rapid growth of the Lebanese Muslim communities brought about by the arrival of refugees and the emerging Lebanese sectarian consciousness in Sydney increased the symbolic and political importance of the position of shaikh. Religious leadership and control of the mosque became a vital means of differentiating Lebanese sectarian identity in Australian urban society. The growth of the community and in the number of associations saw the issue of religious leadership emerge as a question of community prestige. Leadership of the mosque became a key position in the presentation of Sunni Lebanese interests in the context of Lebanese sectarianism and Australian multiculturalism.

The Lebanese Muslim Association, the name of the mosque association, became an encompassing organisation constituted by representatives from Sunni village and city associations in Lebanon. Its growth, and the building of a new mosque in the heart of the Lebanese Sunni communities, saw the role of shaikh quickly change from one that was largely ritual and spiritual to that of a religious and community leader. The new mosque (Imam Ali Mosque), funded by donations from the Sunni community and the Saudi Arabian Ministry of Religious Affairs which contributed approximately $300,000, symbolised the increasing importance of religious identity and prestige in ethnic politics.[12]

The growing cultural and political significance of the mosque brought about a crisis over mosque leadership which saw the incumbent shaikh deposed in an election by Shaikh Zeidan, a new Lebanese shaikh who had attended Al Azhar University, an esteemed centre of Islamic learning in Cairo. The position of imam of the new mosque, was seen to require someone far more prestigious than Shaikh Chami and someone politically more capable of competing on equal terms with the new Maronite bishop in the ethnic political arena.[13] *Shaikh Zeidan was also regarded as politically more attuned to the views and experiences of the new wave of Sunni immigrants and refugees who had been shaped by the politics of the civil war. He had strong links to the Iraqi Ba'th party that was influential amongst the Arab nationalists in north Lebanon at the time.*

Shaikh Zeidan succeeded in gaining the position of imam through village association politics in the mosque association. A village faction from Daniyya had invited the shaikh to visit Sydney and had promoted him in the Sunni community. The shaikh himself came from the same village, which lies just north of Tripoli. Initially the mosque itself had resembled other village and city associations in its social and welfare activities. Welfare work was regarded as a meritorious activity which brought respect and status to those who undertook it and a major focus of associational competition. Community self-help was rewarded through government grants for welfare projects and services and educational activities and associations competed vigorously for it.

For sometime the mosque association remained in competition with the largest Sunni association, the Tripoli al-Mina Association, in the provision of welfare services. This placed the position of imam squarely in the arena of community leadership measured by success in obtaining grants. The Imam was thus not only a religious guide and guardian of tradition, but one who could 'represent' the community.

Representation became a major political issue in the religious politics of the Lebanese in Sydney. Amongst the Muslims this produced tensions between those clerics who had mosques and those who did not. In the words of the original home-grown Sunni cleric Shaikh Chami; 'In Sydney, an imam is a shaikh with a mosque.' Within both Sunni and Shi'i mosque associations this led to ruptures which produced rival leaderships creating numerous 'unemployed shaikhs' supported by different village associations and different international backers. The uncertainty of religious employment at the mosque and inconsistency of the Department of Immigration and Ethnic Affairs in granting permanent resident status to some shaikhs and not others led to protracted conflicts over religious leadership in the Shi'i and Sunni communities.[14]

After five years Shaikh Zeidan found himself under challenge over the issue of community representation. The emergence of radical Islamic movements in Lebanon as a fall-out of the Iranian Islamic revolution, the 1982 Israeli invasion and the disintegration of Lebanese society saw a more fundamentalist Egyptian shaikh, Tajjudin al-Hilaly successfully challenged the incumbent imam.[15] Shaikh Zeidan had *become increasingly unpopular because of his pro-Iraqi Ba'th ties and his close association with powerful Maronite Lebanese leaders. This was graphically demonstrated in his willingness to always be present at those sectarian statements of community religious harmony – the photo opportunity of Lebanese community unity.*[16] *The mosque community increasingly saw him as beholden to a powerful Maronite figure, Eddie Obeid, who aspired to speak for the entire 'Lebanese' community in Australia.*

Politically his Iraqi Ba'th links had drawn him closer to the Maronites and the Kata'ib, motivated by an anti-Syrian sentiment. Shaikh Zeidan's subsequent career was in fact built upon these same links. He eventually became an imam of a new mosque funded by the Iraqi government and maintained his Maronite links. In 1990 during the Gulf crisis he joined a Lebanese delegation to Iraq which sought the release of Australians detained by President Saddam Hussein. The delegation, described at the time as 'Arab Australians', was in fact an anti-Syrian coalition which included a prominent Lebanese Maronite businessman and publisher of a Lebanese and Arab newspaper (el Telegraph), a Maronite who edited a pro-Iraqi Ba'thist newspaper (an-Nahar) and the Maronite Bishop of Sydney.[17] *The Maronite bishop was forced to withdraw at the last minute as a result of political criticism by the Kata'ib of his acceptance of the designation 'Arab' – a strongly-held Maronite myth of origin holds that they are not Arab.*

Shaikh al-Hilaly, by contrast, came out of the new radical Sunni politics of Tawhid which dominated Tripoli between 1983–86. He identified with a radical and assertive Sunni Islam which admired the achievements of Khomeini's revolutionary ideology and supported Sunni/Shi'i ecumenicism. Among the mainly north Lebanese Sunni immigrants support for his candidature was enormous. The electoral contest for the position of imam sparked such interest that the membership of mosque association grew to an all time record. On polling day the queue of eligible voters stretched four blocks and the time had to be extended to allow everyone to vote.

The ascendancy of Shaikh al-Hilaly was a cause of dismay among the Maronite political organisations, as well as diplomatic representatives from several Arab governments. A 10-year campaign to deport him ensued. Each time the imam applied to the Department of Immigration and Ethnic Affairs for permanent residency the Department was lobbied to deport him on the grounds of stirring disharmony in the Lebanese community. The government response was to issue him with a visa renewable on an annual basis and to keep him under close surveillance. This only served to intensify the resentment felt by much of the Sunni community and their efforts to mobilise support for his continuation as imam, even though many were not entirely sympathetic to all his religious views.

But it was the actions of a rival Muslim body, not a Lebanese political party, which almost saw him deported. His address to a group of Muslim university students in which he attacked Israel and Jews was videoed and handed over to the local Jewish Board of Deputies. The imam was accused of breaking laws on racial vilification and came under widespread criticism in the Australian press and parliament. However, he survived and was eventually granted resident status.

A similar pattern of clerical recruitment took place in the Lebanese Shi'i community. Interestingly the politics of recruitment of the first Shi'i shaikh in the late 1970s focused on the tension between secularism and sectarianism in the politics of the Lebanese National Movement and not on Islamic Shi'i radicalism stimulated by the Iranian revolution or the Israeli military occupation of South Lebanon or Beirut after 1982.

Shi'i Secular and Religious Leadership

The largest Shi'i association (around 600 members) at that time was the South Lebanese Association, a strongly secular (or non-sectarian) organisation that identified with the Lebanese National Movement. Many of its members were also Communists and pro-Palestinian. Only in the early 1980s did the politics of the Shi'i mosque shift to a struggle between Amal and Hizbollah. Like Sunni clerics Shaikh Zeidan and Shaikh Hilaly the first Shi'i shaikh, Shaikh Mehdi, was recruited through village community networks. At that time there was no Shi'i cleric to function as a religious guide and the Shi'a drew on the services of the Lebanese Sunni shaikhs.

Because neither of the two main Shi'i community associations at the time, the South Lebanese Association (SLA) and the Islamic Shi'i Association, had sponsored this shaikh there was some ambivalence towards his presence. Part of the difficulty was the fact that his closest Lebanese connections in Australia were in fact a Maronite pro-Kata'ib family from South Lebanon in whose house he was staying. None of the Shi'i community leaders felt they could visit him there given the political connections with the Kata'ib.

Eventually the two associations agreed to meet the shaikh in a neutral public space, the local state primary school. The meeting lasted two hours and provoked several heated exchanges. One particularly uncomfortable moment was when the issue of donations came up. It was considered shameful to be discussing money in front of the shaikh. However, the reality was that unless the associations could demonstrate they could provide sufficient funds to support the shaikh then there was little likelihood that he could obtain a resident's visa to remain in Australia.

Failure to raise the money would be publicly shameful for the community and the shaikh. Firstly he would have to go home because of lack of community support and secondly, given the Sunni cleric Shaikh Zeidan had paid a visit to Shaikh Mehdi a community snub would bring double shame on them.

Those in the SLA reasoned that they needed a shaikh and that one who was indebted to them for his position would be better than one sponsored by the religious hierarchy in Lebanon or Iran. By taking up his application and using the Australian political networks they had developed as a result of the politicisation of sect with the Lebanese civil war the SLA leaders were able to secure Shaikh Mehdi a resident's visa.

Personal attacks against 'leaders', people who 'represented' communities, not only addressed the Lebanese communities, thereby sharpening boundaries between immigrants, but also addressed the status of the Lebanese in the wider multicultural society. Sect was used to distinguish between desirable and undesirable Lebanese migrants. To protect their 'good name', the older Christian Lebanese sought to distance themselves from the recent arrivals. The politicisation of sectarian identity occurred not merely because of ideological or political baggage from the civil war but because of 'proximity' and a 50 per cent increase in the number of Lebanese Muslims – from 23.2 to 33.2 per cent of the Lebanese-born population between 1976–81 – had an immediate impact on the public image of the Lebanese in Australia.

The old Christian Lebanese were in shock that their long struggle for respectability and assimilation was threatened overnight by the arrival of the refugees, especially the large number of Muslims among them. It was they, after all, who had challenged Australian racism early in the century and succeeded in having themselves officially recognised as 'non-Asiatic' to achieve citizenship. As William Abourizk argued in a letter to the Australian prime minister in 1914 '… Syrians are Caucasian and they are a white race as much as the English. Their looks, habits, customs, religion, blood … are those of Europeans, but they are more intelligent ….'[18] In fact many third generation Christian Lebanese felt that their assimilation had gone so far that they were in danger of losing their ethnic identities altogether.[19]

The struggle of the earlier Christian Lebanese migrants articulated a different kind of community from the recent arrivals. The second generation middle class Lebanese commanded a much broader range of financial, political and cultural resources to tell their story. The lobbying of government ministers, parliamentarians, senior bureaucrats and the media allowed them to define the significance of sect in the multicultural arena. The issue of community reputation was translated into the broader arena of ethnic politics. Self-respect and charitable works were projected onto the broader social canvas as measures of community prestige and worth.

The Lebanese refugees were seen as a liability by the older Lebanese migrants and as bringing down the good name of the Lebanese. In the wider Australian society the refugees were also seen as a problem group with many settlement problems. They had few marketable skills, suffered from chronic high unemployment, had little knowledge of English and brought the politics and divisions of the civil war to Sydney. Government bureaucracies and agencies found them fragmented, competitive and difficult to deal with. A frequent complaint was that there were too many associations and leaders! This bad 'image' merely served to emphasise the utility of sect and cultural divisions as a way of differentiating the 'desirable' – and therefore deserving – from the 'undesirable' Lebanese.

Sect and the Good Migrant

In September 1981 the 'Australian Lebanese Committee', in conjunction with the World Lebanese Cultural Union, celebrated 100 years of Lebanese presence in Australia. The event was described in the programme as '... without doubt the most important event in the History of the Lebanese people in Australia'[20] *and was attended by an impressive list of guests including the state premier of New South Wales, ambassadors, leading Australian academics, federal and state politicians, Lebanese government officials and a 'who's who' of the most successful Lebanese families in Australia. It conveyed the image of the Lebanese as a long established, well-to-do and well-connected community able to celebrate its centenary of immigration and settlement in one of the most prestigious venues in Sydney, the Hilton Hotel. The conference was even co-sponsored by the two national airlines, Middle East Airlines and Qantas whose respective mottoes 'Fly with a Smile*

– Lebanon is Our Home' and 'The Airline for All Australians' suggested harmonious union.

However, just as the Australian National Bicentennial in 1988 amounted to a celebration of the most privileged group in Australian society – the descendants of English colonial settlers (even those of convict heritage!) – so too the Lebanese centenary marked the arrival of the old Christian Lebanese, especially Maronite families. The focus of celebration was the arrival of the people from Kfarsghab, a small Maronite village in north. In the context of recent Lebanese immigration from war-torn Lebanon, which had radically changed the social and religious character of the Lebanese communities, it was a celebration of the successful and influential.

The celebration of Christian Maronite Lebanese identity occurred at a time when the communities had been mobilised by the Lebanon war to assist new immigrant co-religionists in settlement and to identify more closely with the politics and divisions of Lebanon. The celebration of a long and successful settlement by a small section of the Lebanese community added legitimacy to their claims for personal recognition and respect as well as the right to speak for the 'Lebanese' in Australia. Politically, it was an attempt by one section of the Australian Lebanese to assert their pre-eminence in community affairs by appropriating the historical discourse on the identity of Lebanese immigrants. They, as successful and established migrants, also assumed the right to speak on behalf of all Lebanese as an ethnic group. In their view respectability and success had been the hallmark of the Lebanese immigrant story. The centennial celebration and the assembled audience were concrete affirmation of this.

Government recognition of reputation also comes in the form of community welfare grants. Successful applications for grants confer prestige on associations and respectability in the wider society. The state's policy of opening up the discourse on cultural pluralism has had the effect of circumscribing what and who is socially acceptable by reward and denial. Thus Lebanese sectarianism, transformed by the politics of the civil war, became entangled in the politics of incorporation and acceptance into Australian society.

However, within the Lebanese Sunni and Shi'i communities the question of religious identity has not been circumscribed by the rivalry of old and new immigrants. Community space is not only delineated by the intersection between sectarian identity and class status but by the confrontation between religious movements and Western secular institutions in the Muslim world and Orientalist disdain for Muslim culture. The politics of Muslim immigrant acceptance has been experienced by many as an extension of this struggle in the West. In the Western industrial city 'Islam' has found itself under siege. Ritual practice, etiquette, dress codes, law and morality are all the subject of scrutiny by the wider society. Muslim immigrant response to uninvited media attention and constant critiques of Muslim culture has been to engage in a defence of cultural authenticity. 'We are misunderstood.' 'People say things are Islamic which have nothing to do with Islam.'

What they experience as cultural siege has drawn many into the definition and defence of orthodoxy – what is really Islamic and what is not. Orthodoxy as defence denies the multiplicity of meanings all practices potentially have. The wearing of the headscarf has become a symbol of religious identity both for women, and for men. Muslim women 'representatives' argue for the scarf's cultural authenticity, even adapting feminist discourse against the treatment of women as sexual ornaments to the wearing of *hijab*: 'I feel very comfortable in these clothes, they conceal me and deny men from making a sex object of me.'

In universities, the pressure to conform to cultural orthodoxy is felt by women students. Through the accidents of immigration, and the multiculturalism which tends to make Arabic language the province of second generation Arab immigrants, the classroom has become a space to enforce symbolic conformity. Muslim female students are often pressured to wear the veil by their Muslim male class mates.

Conformity is a source of reassurance and support, identifying membership and revaluing tradition. Communal ritual reinforces identity in a culture under siege. Of the five precepts or pillars of faith – belief in the oneness of God, prayer, fasting, the pilgrimage – prayer and fasting have become the most visible public expressions of faith in Sydney.

Flexibility becomes less as transgressions and failures of practice are interpreted as disloyalty to the community and even personal weakness. The recommended five times a day prayer becomes mandatory and is taken up as a major issue of discrimination in cases where employers do not provide the opportunity for their Muslim workers to fulfil the obligation. In one case a Lebanese Muslim employee with the State Rail Authority was sacked, accused of using prayer as an excuse to shirk his duties.[21]

In Sydney communal prayer at the mosque has also assumed an important public character expressing religious unity. Communal prayer has always had an important egalitarian and unifying function in Islam, but in migration it has the additional role of identifying a sectarian minority. The Imam Ali mosque built at Lakemba provided a focal point for settlement and for public worship for Lebanese Sunni Muslims.

The other precept of faith which has become an important public symbol of Muslim identity in Australia, even amongst those who pray irregularly or fail to observe the prohibition on alcohol, is the fast. In fact, fasting during Ramadan among Lebanese Sunni immigrants has had a popular revival. To non-Muslims it is a very conspicuous act of self-denial, most apparent in schools and the work place. Not only is it noticed, but in many cases it has to be accommodated – allowances made – within the daily routines of school life and factory production. While not all authorities are tolerant of the practice – one primary school teacher ridiculed a Muslim student's fast as a 'disgusting diet' [22]– others are forced to accept the fact that the daily breaking of the fast will occur at sunset and not at some convenient break in production and that there will be mass absenteeism among Muslim workers at Id al-fitr, a traditional Muslim holiday marking the end of Ramadan.

Other ritual practices which have become important are the consumption of *halal* meat and Islamic burial. The case of *halal* meat is interesting. Formerly a difficult practice to fulfil except by private slaughtering – which led to frequent criticism of Muslim families in the suburbs – the development of a Middle East meat export trade, has made *halal* – killed meat readily available to immigrant Muslim communities and more acceptable to the Australian public. Underlining this new-found tolerance, the Australian Livestock and Meat Corporation sponsored delegations and Muslim clergy from different Middle East countries to study the procedures for *halal* slaughtering. Now the number of Muslim slaughtermen in Australian abattoirs is so numerous that even the Australian public gets to eat *halal* meat unwittingly.

The demarcation of community space through communal ritual necessitates a geographical concentration of Muslims – the mutual reinforcement of being seen – and the social availability of men for Friday prayer. While some men are able and willing to organise Friday off work to attend the mosque, in most cases attendance is a function of their economic commitments. The congregation of Friday prayer is largely a population of retired or unemployed men, or shopkeepers who can leave their shops in the hands of family members, often wives.

The mosque becomes the centre of participation in the religious community. Important festivals of the religious calendar, such as Id al-Fitr, Mohammed's birthday, or the Muslim new year, have become occasions to display religious support and ethnic political influence. The annual attendance at the Id al-Fitr celebrations at the Imam Ali

Mosque in Lakemba is regularly around 15,000 Lebanese Sunni Muslims. Too large for the mosque, the congregation overspills into the road way where the service is broadcast on loud speakers.

The mosque is also the focal point of the defence of cultural authenticity and is linked to Middle Eastern clerical concerns over the decay of Islam in the West. An important dimension of Ayatollah Khomeini's *fatwa* against Salman Rushdie's book *The Satanic Verses* was precisely over the fear of apostasy among the growing number of Muslim immigrants in the West. Losing 'believers' is a fear of all immigrant minority religions.

The mosque is a community space which directly and uniquely addresses believers. While ideologically conceived as an egalitarian space which all believers are welcome to attend in practice, the constitution of the mosque is the product of ethnic appropriation of urban space and the formation of community through reference to parochial identities of place, family and sect. In the case of the Lebanese Sunni their mosque (Imam Ali) is dominated by people from Tripoli while the Lebanese Shi'i mosque (al-Zahra) is attended by people from border villages from South Lebanon. Religiously the ethnic and regional character of these mosques is an expression of the local autonomy of community religious life, largely independent of wider organisational and bureaucratic structures. The Imam is both leader and religious guide of a minority faith in a multicultural environment.

One expression of this autonomy is the insistence by mosque associations of holding onto ethnic/national identifiers in their names. Despite efforts by the Australian Federation of Islamic Councils (AFIC), the national body based on mosque associations, to prohibit the inclusion of ethnic/national identifiers, this has been successfully resisted.[23]

The Sunni Imam's sermons and the casual meeting of the congregation reinforces a highly specific cultural world, the view of immigrants from north Lebanon in dialogue with an imam formed by its recent turbulent politics and interested in ecumenical relations between Sunni and Shi'i Islam. Events in Lebanon and the Middle East are constant topics in sermons as well as personal exchanges. The issues raised include the treatment of the Palestinians in Lebanon, the moral hypocrisy of the Saudi royal family, the injustices of the Arab–Israeli peace process, the contradictions of Algerian democratisation and the corruption of Lebanese politicians. When Australian politicians are invited to attend feast days at the mosque much is made of their pro-Arab sympathies and understanding.[24] The historical grievances of Lebanese Muslims and the victimhood of colonialism and imperialism are the lenses through which current events are interpreted. The voicing of this memory in the mosque connects cultural memory with their current social predicament – a minority suffering discrimination and experiencing very high levels of unemployment.

The relevance of events in the Middle East to their immigrant identities is articulated through public declarations, sometimes in the form of demonstrations and sometimes through spokespeople in the media. The defence is one of fairness – 'we are not responsible for events in the Middle East, why blame us?' – and of misrepresentation.

But the very basis of media communication limits the possibility of understanding, in part because of its highly visual character.[25] Presence in the media, in the eyes of viewers, is reduced to symbolic association in a story about Islam whose parameters are already set. A headscarf symbolises the 'ethnic Muslim' point of view. It confirms religious conservatism, patriarchal values and a bundle of attitudes and opinions about the 'problems with Muslims' as ghettoised communities. The mosque signifies an alien cultural presence and long robes, beard and cap Muslim religious fanaticism. Rarely are such symbols challenged, merely deployed as building blocks in restating the Islamic story.

Immigrants themselves experience similar problems in their

acquisition of knowledge about their own cultures. Distant from the institutions, expertise and cultural mediums which transmit knowledge, they receive and recreate cultural knowledge in disconnected spaces in a social condition which culturally deskills them. Religious knowledge is transmitted in the mosque or at home in Arabic, which is quickly degraded across generations. Orthodoxy, knowledge about what is authentic Muslim belief and practice, is itself honed by the defence of simplified versions of Islamic rules. Under siege, knowledge contracts to points which can be defended. Islam is claimed as an unchanging tradition and fundamentalist formulations simplifying religious experience are accepted while knowledge about Islamic history, about the development of Islamic law and its diversity and even the history of Islamic institutions in Lebanon is unknown or disappears. Moreover, little is known of the diversity of social movements in Islamic countries.

Immigrants are connected beyond the local community through new transnational religious forms. The internationalisation of Islam as a reassertive transnational movement is, of course, ethical and political, but it is also heavily dependant on visual forms – on the communication of events encapsulated as sequences of meaningful Islamic symbols. The protests of Shi'i Muslims in Sydney over *The Satanic Verses* were therefore not so much an expression of Hizbollah demands in Sydney, as a sympathetic response to images received from elsewhere which give identity to a small community. This was tellingly revealed in the interviews with demonstrators who could barely explain their rage, had no knowledge of the offending text, and echoed only the text of Khomeini's *fatwa* or the responses of militant imams elsewhere. The way the demonstrators were easily trapped by journalists into declaring their willingness to murder Rushdie, even though they were unlikely to have even considered the possibility, echoed responses they themselves had seen on the media and understood as the correct Islamic response.

The mosque as community in immigration is constructed from

the urban process, the direct appropriation of social space, but also as an internationally connected space whose cultural communication is condensed into symbols. Thus the sense of community constructed here is the connection between localities in what Fischer calls hybridised cultural forms. Generated not just through communal rituals but a ' ... wide variety of communicative channels'.[26]

Extending command over social space in this case is not based on the ability to convert cultural capital and enter a different kind of community, middle class or even national, but to be part of an international and localised community. Transnational Islamic symbols, sharpened by their controversial edge in the West, become a vehicle for new cultural and political connections based on reductive knowledges of tradition, but evoking a consciousness of 'imagination' which is 'national'.

Conclusion

In the urban space of the industrial city the ideology of incorporation has always been assimilation. That people had the right, in Rieff's words, '... to opt out of the continuum of history, choosing isolation over community, and one's desires over one's obligations.'[27] Immigrants have constructed communities appropriate to the urban space they occupy. The re-creation of ties of social reciprocity is not merely continuity but the basis of class location in the city. Identity politics which engage local knowledge – the intimacies of social biographies and the surveillance of others – serve to differentiate people. Often interpreted as 'ghettoisation' and expressing separatist sentiment, identity politics represent a mode of existence and identity allocated to them in urban space. Identity is not merely a question of authenticity and difference, but a political question of evaluation of acceptance. The multicultural city has proposed difference as the basis of incorporation.

6

Islam, Multiculturalism and the Global City

In the radically fragmented, heterogeneous world of the future, a world of mobility, contingency, and isolation, the radically fragmented city of Los Angeles believed it would find a comfortable – and profitable niche. 'We're a collage city … that's not such a bad thing to be in a collage world.'[1]

Islam (tradition) in the global city is a product of the international mobility of people and their social incorporation through the urban process. In Australia Lebanese Muslim immigrants were a displaced proletariat whose reliance on family and community was a strategy of urban subsistence. Recreating community was the social basis of organisation and identity in a multicultural urban space. Multiculturalism, in turn, was an expression of the social fragmentation of the city and its global connections. The collage city created through migration was an ' … anthology of the world'.[2] Islam is part of that modern anthology and an expression of the new forms of social consciousness in the city.

Islam in Australia was constituted as one of a plurality of ethnic cultures whose social roots were established through the national programme of mass immigration from the mid-twentieth century. This project of recruiting people internationally to fulfil capital's demands for labour produced an unanticipated social result. 'White Australia', the idea that one could make Australians out of culturally diverse migrants by teaching them English and putting them to work, had to be abandoned in 1975 in the face of the social reality of cultural pluralism in the city.

State recognition of pluralism was not just a crisis in national identity – the pretence of the national myth of whiteness – but one of the social regulation of a culturally diverse immigrant working class. The official multiculturalism was introduced in response to the crisis of assimilation and social mobility, the problem of Non English-Speaking immigrant culture being synonymous with disadvantage and isolation. Multiculturalism recognises the processes of pluralisation, which are not peculiar to the Australian case. Throughout cities in the North international labour migration has gone hand in hand with the official recognition of pluralism and the retreat from the state's commitment to a social wage based on individual social, political and civil rights. Legislation aimed at protecting 'group rights' – affirmative action, racial vilification – while expressed in terms of collective disadvantage and tolerance conceals the nature and conditions of the post-modern urban proletariat.

Multiculturalism and Urban Consciousness

'Multiculturalism' represents a shift of the imagining of community from national to urban space. Migrants neither assimilated nor dispersed throughout the country but instead concentrated overwhelmingly – around 80 per cent of them – in the two major cities of Sydney and Melbourne. These were the major sites of investment and domestic growth sustained by labour inflows and new consumers. It was the city landscape that had become multicultural, not the nation, with some suburbs having up to half their residents born overseas.

Multiculturalism, the creation of a culturally diverse non English-speaking working class with special needs, was a consequence of 'demand-side-urbanisation', the focus on the city as a locus for investment in a built environment. In Australia rapid urbanisation was directly linked to globalisation, the international mobility of capital and labour. The political expectation was that the modern city would liberate immigrants from old ways and attachments. The New World promise of success through individual effort was an integral part of the national project of incorporation.

The significance of the recognition of multiculturalism in the city is not that it names something new but sees something that always existed. The industrial city was always a culturally plural domain formed by an immigrant population drawn from its hinterland or from more geographically remote parts. The official naming of pluralism signals the abandonment of the assumptions of modernity – namely that urbanisation would bring about the radical transformation of the individual either through emancipation and selfhood, or through the realisation of a radical class consciousness. It abandons the city as the centrepiece for cultural standardisation in the nation.

Multiculturalism declares a new role for the city in the process of the social incorporation of people, making difference instead of sameness its basis. It creates social categories of belonging which are assumed to be equivalent but which in practice are not. This is particularly evident in Australia where 'migrant' was shorthand for non-English speaking members of the unskilled working class. The celebration of cultures in this case was the celebration of working class cultures while cultural differences were manifestations of strategies of settlement and structures of opportunity rather than the way people lived and understood the world.

The political economy of multiculturalism lies at the nexus of income and social reciprocity, which constitute for many immigrant workers urban subsistence. The new patterns of marginal employment and increased family and community reliance are the proletarian forms of the global city. They constitute not only forms of self reliance but also the potential for continued mobility. Just as global capital has no attachments so labour has created social forms for mobility. 'A worker with extensive kinship obligations may use them to command geographical mobility rather than to remain locked in place.'[3] Of course the utility of such cultural capital for mobility varies enormously from to community to community and family to family. The uncertainties of migration – will I stay? will I return home? will I move on? – are simply reinforced within these cultural fragments. However, this mobility is between similar social spaces, communities created out of the subsistence strategies of the urban and rural poor in different parts of the world.

Travel between communities allows individuals to take advantage of discrepancies in the value of cultural capital, labour and commodities. But it is rarely transformative and does not generally allow them to convert cultural capital into other forms of durable social advantage. Good incomes in Australia allow families to care for aged parents in Lebanon by hiring a Sri Lankan maid (even during the war), smuggling illegal goods between Lebanon and Australia may make buying a house easier, arranging a marriage can fulfil family commitments by converting kinship ties into citizenship rights and citizenship rights, in turn, may provide access to cheap good quality higher education (unaffordable in Lebanon) and new employment opportunities.[4]

Multiculturalism is not purely descriptive of ethnic cultures but a social naming which also tends to homogenise. In other words, multiculturalism homogenises difference and thereby helps make ethnic culture something to transact over. From the perspective of the state, the homogenisation of 'ethnic culture' makes it more organised and manageable. The controversy over the local mosques employing and sacking their imams and the government frustration over not being able to deal with a more centralised and bureaucratised church-like structure is a case in point. From the perspective of the communities the claim to representation constitutes the group and gives it leverage in ethnic politics. It is significant that multiculturalism post-dates the nation state because its expression is contingent upon the existence of the model of the nation state. Ethnic culture is an 'imagined community' like the nation state but it is peoplehood constructed without the accompanying state.

There is another sense in which ethnic cultures post-date the nation state. In Australia most ethnic cultures are generally derivative expressions of it – except in those cases where 'people' have not yet realised a nation state (e.g. Palestinians, Kurds, Assyrians). Most immigrant ethnic cultures, whether Greek, Italian, Egyptians or Argentinians, are 'myths', 'communities' constructed out of national communities. But all immigrants, even those who do not accept their national identification, were already 'nationals', proletarianised and made members of nation states before they migrated. In the post-colonial world transnational migrations dispersed other nationals around the world.

Multiculturalism describes a different system of social categorisation in the post-modern city which is the product of an interactive process of official naming and community self-identification. This makes it a highly contested process because the outcome delineates social power and social worth. Identity becomes something to transact over because it determines who can represent whom. A recent dramatic display of this in Australia is the crisis over the Australian government's decision to officially rename an ethnic group who had long identified themselves as Macedonians as 'Slav–Macedonians'. Successful protests by a large and influential Greek ethnic lobby after Australia's diplomatic recognition of the new state of Macedonia led to the government renaming.[5] The official renaming contradicted the long-standing policy of a culturally much more sensitised part of the bureaucracy dealing with ethnic cultural affairs, the Special Broadcasting Service, which provides ethnic radio and television programming. They accept 'self-description' of ethnic groups on the basis of social and cultural identification. To have done otherwise would have engendered enormous political conflict between official and denied nationalisms such as those of Palestinians or Kurds.

The category 'Lebanese' as an Australian ethnic identity remains highly contested as a category of representation. 'Lebanese' had once been constructed around the acceptance, success and respectability of Christian Lebanese over two and three generations.[6] The arrival of the Lebanese Muslims under the circumstances of war and unemployment undermined this image. As the established Christian Lebanese generally saw it, the category 'Lebanese' was degraded by the arrival of the Muslim Lebanese.

Multiculturalism, however, refers not only to a category but also to social space. Specifically for migrants it involves the 'ethnicisation' of urban space through the formation of community. The recreation of community based upon social reciprocities is symptomatic of the lack of the cultural and financial capital to command space differently. Multiculturalism represents a new form of urban consciousness in which self reliance and state clientism of ethnic groups is a means of social regulation. The response of respectable community 'representatives', both Christian and Muslim, to the 'bad name' given Lebanese because of high employment and dependence on social welfare is an example. The solution they offered was to personally evaluate the claims themselves. They suggested waiting outside Social Security offices and questioning any Lebanese who came through the doors about the reasons why they could not find work; and they would recommend withdrawing benefits from those they believed were 'sponging off the system'. In this way respected members of the Lebanese community could protect the 'good' name of the community by penalising the 'bad' individuals. While the two projects of producing ethnic culture – the official and the community – are different they are mutually dependent and exploitative. From the official perspective the formation of community in ethnicised urban space confirms the centrality of cultural identity amongst immigrants, while from the perspective of immigrants, the official homogenising constructions of multiculturalism can be used by 'community' representatives both to legitimate their political claims to speak for others and to constitute the group.[7] Positive discrimination policies are one example of the way state intervention directly constructs cultures and reinforces categories, for they establish the parameters in terms of which claims of discrimination and racism can be made as collective claims.

Islam and Multiculturalism

While the official discourse on ethnic culture is homogenising, the actual production of 'ethnic culture' in community space is partial and fragmentary. The very context of the cultural reproduction of language, history, social memory and religious knowledge is impoverished. Family becomes the major space for recreating knowledge, memory and cultural skills. Language is in most cases reproduced as a shrunken domestic idiom. History is contained within family memory and perhaps at the Saturday language school, in sermons at the mosque, or in the ethnic constructions of the Arabic press. Illiteracy and reverence for Arabic as a sacred language can also conspire to make the Qur'an a symbolic object to be hung on a wall but never read (and never touched by non-believers) for fear of mispronouncing the 'Word of God'.[8] Even amongst Muslim immigrants who are recognised in the community as cultural authorities and able to authenticate Islamic culture this can be the case. Locally grown Lebanese shaikhs often present Islamic Law, the Shari'a, as unchangeable and comprehensive – apparently unaware that their own knowledge of it is the eclectic heritage of the Ottoman family law reform of 1917 which subsequently became the basis of Sunni Family Law in Lebanon.

Central to cultural reproduction and community identity are narratives about Muslim experience in the contemporary world, as Arabs, as Lebanese, as Muslims and as immigrants. The discourse on identity is globalised by the very experience of migration. The narratives of their experience traverse socialisation, parochial sectarianism in a Lebanon witnessing national disintegration, incorporation as immigrants in Australia and a new consciousness as members of a global Muslim community. This broad experience is collapsed into the question of why Muslims continue to be the underdogs. Explanation is found in the belief of the continuing antipathy of the West towards Islam and the historical victimhood of Muslims, especially in the twentieth century.

Lebanese Muslim immigrants experience the whole process of community formation and cultural production as an historical continuation of Western antagonism to Islam. Muslim cultural practices and knowledge are constantly criticised in the Australian press, by media commentators and government agencies. Some of these issues are formulated in terms of the assumptions of the colonial encounter, '... civilisation must come from abroad'.[9] Translated into the experience of labour migration from the South to the North it assumes that the integration of immigrants can only take place through values acceptable to the dominant culture. The Australian Family Law Council's recommendations on legislation against clitoridectomy resemble colonial 'repugnancy laws' and the focus on veiling as symbolic of Muslim women's oppression continues the long-standing dialogue over civilisational superiority and the right cultural intervention.[10] Just as racism and colonialism were historically closely linked as a mode of intervention and regulation, so too are racism and cultural differentiation amongst immigrants in the North.

The Muslim immigrant response – at least from those who assume the position of representatives – is to seek refuge in cultural authenticity as a defence against racism. Imams, shaikhs and respected Muslims assume the role of cultural guardians claiming the exclusive right to speak about their 'cultural property' and determine what is valid or invalid as practice. Practices and values attributed to Muslims – such as female circumcision, veiling, violence, fanaticism, unwillingness to work – become a focus for the defence of Islam. Orthodoxy becomes a defended cultural space of those symbolic behaviours that visibly mark off a Muslim identity in a multicultural environment. Cultural authentication produces a debate which is more about what is not Islamic than the reverse. In the process a critique of the social conditions of Muslim proletarianisation is forgotten and the habitus of cultural practices ignored.

The claim to be uniquely capable of speaking for oneself has consequences within broader Australian institutions and fields of knowledge. Representation and cultural authenticity extend the domain to all discussions of culture. Even universities become the object of cultural authentication by culturally approved spokespersons. 'Others' – those without the appropriate ethnic or cultural attributes – are charged with Orientalism. The teaching of Arabic is an example. The subject provides 'native speakers' (immigrants with Arabic speaking backgrounds) with the possibility of employment as interpreters and translators in the courts and the bureaucracy, or as teachers in the secondary school system. Arabic then is cultural capital, produced in domestic and community space, which can be transposed into educational and vocational advantage in the wider society in the provision of service to immigrants. Arabic language classes in Sydney's universities are consequently attended overwhelmingly by first and second generation Arab Australians. Language learning becomes closely associated with the material needs of the Arabic speaking immigrant working class – the provision of interpreters and translators to guarantee Arabic speakers who have little or no English equity in their dealings with state bureaucracies and agencies. It's significance in multicultural Australia is not primarily as the sacred language of the Qur'an, or of a great world literature, or even as an important trading language, but as a language of a particularly disadvantaged group.

The Arab students are invariably highly critical of the quality and content of courses – sometimes, no doubt, with good reason. However, the issue is who should be the proper teacher, the proper transmitter of cultural knowledge. Thus teachers are criticised for their national background (especially Lebanese against Egyptians and vice-versa), because they are of the wrong gender, religion or because their standard of Arabic is poor. In isolated cases fundamentalist male students have made demands to change courses and teaching personnel, and to monopolise interpretations of culture and history according to very narrow religious positions. In one case, Muslim women students were pressured to wear headscarves and a campaign was waged for the dismissal of a teacher because she was a woman and a Christian. The campaigners believed that she was incapable of providing adequate instruction in Arabic or Islamic history and that a fundamentalist shaikh should be invited to lecture instead. The campaign was unsuccessful.

Social research on Muslim communities funded by government agencies is also frequently subjected to the scrutiny of 'community' representatives who sit on the committees which oversee the progress of projects. The policy of appointing such committees is based on the idea of community consultation. One study undertaken by the author ended up in controversy over the issue of publication. The document was not criticised because of research flaws or even bias but because it damaged the name of the Muslim community by revealing its poverty and disadvantage and should not, therefore, be published.[11]

Significantly multicultural identities, while forged in domestic, community and national space connect a variety of spaces internationally. As discussed in earlier chapters, these identities vary in their transnational significance according to their articulation with broader national and transnational identities. As other studies of Muslim immigrant communities in Europe reveal, each community has its distinct social origins, linguistic and often ethnic character.

In addition communities have specific sectarian and regional origin. Thus, for example, in Belgian mosques the Jama'at-i Tabligh from India is very influential, in Britain the *Jama'at-i Islami* is popular amongst the Pakistani communities, in Germany the Turkish Department of Religious Affairs (Diyanet) has strongly shaped religious life alongside other Turkish Islamic movements such as Süleymançi and Milli Görüs and in France the Alawiyya has been influential amongst Algerians.[12]

In immigrant communities many ethnicised urban spaces only connect village communities in the diaspora and not broader political or religious communities. The contrast between Lebanese Maronite and Lebanese Shi'a and Sunni ethnicised spaces is instructive here. While Maronite immigrants will, in many cases, have much greater generational depth in the diaspora and be more widely geographically dispersed they still constitute a small ethnic culture. International Lebanese Maronite organisations such as the Maronite Church and the Lebanese World Cultural Union (predominantly Maronite) exist, but they are limited when compared with the connections of Lebanese Sunni and Shi'a immigrants to Islamic clerical networks, Islamic movements and religious groups. Lebanese Muslim consciousness is formed in the context of local cultural practice as well as a dialogue about Islam and its position in international cultural and political movements. Thus Lebanese Muslims are connected with transnational spaces which include denationalised spaces, nationally 'occupied' spaces, immigrant spaces and village spaces. Lebanese Muslim experience of the disintegration of the Lebanese state, directly or vicariously, saw the sectarian predicament in Lebanon reformulated by radical Islamic movements which claimed a new role and vision for Lebanese society. Religion directly connected them with alternative visions to Lebanese sectarianism and to the Muslim world in general.

Lebanese Muslim experience, whether as a sectarian member of Lebanese society or as a new Australian immigrant, emphasised the social necessity of family and community as integral to proletarian experience. But the dialogue about being Muslim in Australia is also constructed within the context of global communications. While the politics of multiculturalism tends to be homogenising at the local level, the media homogenises Islam at the global level. The instantaneous media world of images impregnates events involving Muslims, Muslim countries and Islamic culture with stereotypes of Islam. The arena of immigrant response, however, is not international but Australian multicultural society. Muslims immigrants find themselves having to defend cultural authenticity as a means to counter the creation of 'global Islamic culture' in the media. The media is, in short, experienced as a source of victimisation and racism towards Muslims.

Global communications technology has tended to reinforce local worlds in two ways. At a personal level telephones facilitate direct contact with family and community allowing the progress and concerns of day-to-day life to be shared. Parallel existences can be lived, directly and vicariously, between members of geographically distant households and communities. Unlike the experience of earlier generations of Lebanese emigrants, such as those to Argentina early this century, today's generation are not physically and socially disconnected from their past lives through the loss of literacy in Arabic.[13] Telephones – with special rates for family and friends overseas as the Australian Telecom advertisement informs us – ensure that personalised worlds can endure by voice. And international computer networks now link the Lebanese diaspora through electronic bulletin boards (e.g. LEBNET) bringing daily news reports, writing commentary on events in Lebanon, publishing personal letters on news and life in Lebanon, providing travel information about cheap air fares to Lebanon and publishing detailed information on local events in Lebanese villages and districts.[14] Video recordings of marriages and family celebrations also provided opportunities for others' vicarious participation in many parts of the world.[15] Television, videos, international computer networks, telecommunication and fast air travel are allowing 'imagined communities' to be constructed through almost instantaneous cultural mediums which no longer depend on mass literacy to achieve cultural standardisation of 'nations'. The new communications reinforce the processes of cultural pluralisation everywhere.

Mass communications also serve to connect Muslims as an aggrieved 'imagined community' globally. In fact this symbiosis between global homogenisation and local resistance has become an integral part of the discourse of multiculturalism at all levels. As part of the enterprise of post-modernity there appears to have developed a collusion between the 'Orientalists and nativists' joining in the same essentialist project but with different purpose.[16]

'Islam' as a global category becomes homogenised by Islamists and Orientalists alike. The Islamists homogenise 'Islam' by reducing the solution to the contemporary crisis in Muslim societies to a utopian vision of individual morality and government in accordance with Shari'a. The Orientalists homogenise 'Islam' by constructing the Muslim 'Other' as anti-West antagonistic to its values of liberalism, secularism and progress. In symbiosis these two projects actually feed on each other fuelling fundamentalist solutions and Western fears.

Locally Muslim immigrants resist the global homogenisation of Islam as anti-Western by demanding equal cultural rights to build mosques, to bury the dead according to Islamic law,[17] and to have cultural practices recognised in law (e.g. make bridewealth (*al-mahr*) an enforceable as a pre-marriage contract). Broader Muslim organisations such as the Islamic Council of New South Wales, a state-wide body in which all mosque associations are represented, have taken up the task of challenging media stereotypes about Islam and Muslims through letters to the editor, publishing examples of stereotyping in community papers such as the *Muslim Times*, and being available for media comment. Media misrepresentation of

Islam is a constant complaint of Muslim immigrants and their organisations.

Resistance to an 'Orientalist' version of Islam is reinforced by the sense of being part of a 'global' Muslim community and new internationalist Islamic currents. The pilgrimage to Mecca, the appointment of overseas imams as religious leaders, visits by eminent overseas clerics, Arabic radio broadcasts of religious sermons and the circulation of the sermons of popular Cairene imams on cassette tapes in the community all contribute to the sense of being part of an active global Muslim community. Events in the Muslim world and their reporting also generate sympathetic responses which engender a sense of belonging to a global Muslim community.[18]

In the Muslim immigrant communities of the global city the category 'Islam' becomes a doubly homogenised concept through which difference is defined within a multicultural discourse. Cultural authenticity defends local community space which then becomes articulated with a broader international cultural politics. In a political and institutional sense the Lebanese Muslim diaspora community space is institutionally largely autonomous. Imams are elected by the community and traditional rights such as the husband's prerogative to declare *talaq* are practised unmediated by state legal institutions as occurs in the Middle East. In addition organisations have developed in the context of migration which are quite unique such as Muslim women's advocacy groups, strongly supported by shaikhs, promoting the special welfare and spiritual needs of women. However, despite this autonomy, the discourse of identity and cultural authenticity tends to limit the number of public Muslim voices. The problem is who can speak in the context of the homogenising of Islam at the local, national and international levels? Silence for the solidarity of community is a defensive strategy here.

It has been argued that the autonomy of the Muslim diaspora in the West – away from the national surveillance of their places of origin – has provided fertile ground for the development of radical Islam.[19] However, the suggested radicalism often turns out to be a dialogue with an homogenised Islamic tradition in which strict rules and discipline are embraced for security. The truncated character of ethnic identity on the one hand, and the sense of uncertainty about futures, close rather than open cultural inquiry. The tendency towards homogenisation by official naming and group politics of representation and solidarity also reinforces closure.

The Lebanese Muslim immigrant experience in Sydney can be replicated in many cities of the industrialised world. The trajectories of social life are not contained within narratives of class, of national membership or individual emancipation. Multiculturalism is a social condition in which people must articulate their identities in dialogue with tradition which is expressed locally, nationally and globally. Pressed into the social forms of urban subsistence in the global city, cultural authenticity has been embraced as something of value to transact over. For Muslim immigrants the *umma* is being reconstructed as social fragments linked to different localities and currents in the Muslim world. Their own insistence on maintaining the ethnic identity of their religious associations indicates that, even amongst themselves, they often find it difficult to put sameness before difference. But unlike the 'imagined community' of the nation which also promised political and cultural autonomy and control over destiny, the 'imagined community' of fragments can only remain and islands to be defended and journeyed between.

Notes

Chapter One

1. Throughout this book stories, anecdotes and case studies are interspersed with the main text. The aim is to insert ethnographic examples in the context of the argument rather than argument in the context of ethnography. The analysis of immigrant lives is not contained within discrete social space such as the village or quarter, and even this was in many respects a functionalist fiction.

2. Political repression and economic crisis in Argentina, a country of mass immigration in the late 19th and early 20th centuries, has led to such large numbers of second and third generation Italians seeking to retrieve the nationality of their parents and grandparents that many Italian consulates outside Buenos Aires were closed down to stem the flow.

3. Sarmiento, Domingo *Civilizacion y Barbarie*, Buenos Aires: Felix Lajoune, 1889.

4. Mass immigration has been a very significant political and social issue in Australia since 1947. Immigration has consistently run at about 1% of population annually. The result is that around 23% of the national population is overseas born and some 70% of post-war national population increase can be attributed to immigrants and their children.

5. There is some irony in this position since the Australian government has, at the same time, been extremely concerned about 'welfare abuse' – i.e. the acquisition of citizenship for the enjoyment of social benefits in Australia or their country of origin.

6. In Australia immigrants are eligible for citizenship after three years continuous residence. They are then entitled to vote.

7. Marshall T. H., *Citizenship and Social Class* and Other Essays, Cambridge: Cambridge University Press 1950.

8. Ibid., p. 20.

9. Barbalet, J. M. *Citizenship: Rights, Struggle and Class Inequality*, Milton Keynes: Open University Press 1988, p. 2.

10. Fischer, Michael M. J. and Mehdi Abedi *Debating Muslims: Cultural Dialogues in Postmodernity and Tradition*, Wisconsin: University of Wisconsin Press 1990, p. 253.

11. Ibid., p. 288. Fischer observes that the US and Europe become major breeding grounds for fundamentalism because of the greater freedom of expression experienced.

12. Harvey, David *The Urban Experience*, Oxford: Basil Blackwell, 1989, pp. 139–40.

13. Ibid., p. 29.

14. Ibid., p. 126.

15. In Australia there have been many examples of state government support to enhance the competitive edge of cities in the past few years. The West Australian government bailed out a major bank – Rothwell's in Perth – to prevent bankruptcy, the Victorian state government paid 30 million dollars to Kodak to prevent a threatened closure of the Australian plant of this multinational and the NSW Government succeeded in attracting the Australian Motorcycle grandprix race away from Victoria by building a new race track in the west of Sydney. In the latter case it was a dispute over the Victorian government's attempt to force the tobacco industry out of the sponsorship of sporting events which provided the NSW Government with the opportunity to steal the race.

16. Harvey op. cit., 1989, p. 48.

17. The term the global city usually refers to the role of key cities in the circuits of capital and the co-ordination of global economic production and services. See Sassen, Saskia *Global Cities*, Princeton: Princeton University Press, 1991. I am broadening the term here to included the impact of the labour market and the pluralisation of cities.

18. Ibid., p. 132.

19. Offe, Claus *Disorganised Capitalism: Contemporary Transformations*

of Work and Politics, Cambridge: Polity Press, 1985.

20. Ibid., pp. 47–8.

21. Spivak, Gayatri Chakravorty *The Postcolonial Critic: Interviews, Strategies and Dialogues*, edited by Sarah Harasym, London & New York: Routledge, 1990, p. 61.

22. Ibid., p. 66.

23 Fussell, Paul *The Great War and Modern Memory*, London, Oxford New York: Oxford University Press, 197, p. 321.

Chapter Two

1. Bourdieu, Pierre 'The Social Space and the Genesis of Groups' *Theory and Society*, 14: 723–44, 1985, p. 724.

2. Soja, Edward *Postmodern Geographies: the Reassertion of Space in Critical Social Theory*, London, New York: Verso, 1989, p. 80.

3. The concept of 'cultural capital' refers to the necessary knowledge (taste and symbolic resources) to occupy a particular social space. Thus for Bourdieu '... the dominant class constitutes a relatively autonomous space whose structure is defined by the distribution of economic and cultural capital among its members, each class fraction being characterised by a certain configuration of this distribution to which there corresponds a certain lifestyle, through the mediation of the habitus' Bourdieu, Pierre *Distinction: A Social Critique of the Judgement of Taste*, London: Routledge Kegan Paul, 1984, p. 260.

4. Soja op. cit. 1989, p. 92.

5. Rieff, David *Los Angeles: Capital of the Third World*, London: Phoenix, 1991, p. 45.

6. Claus Offe in *Disorganised Capitalism: Contemporary Transformations of Work and Politics*, Cambridge: Polity Press 1985, discusses this withdrawal from guaranteeing the social wage with reference to welfare and David Broad in 'Global Economic Restructuring and the Casualisation of Work in the Center: With Canadian Illustrations', *Review*, XIV, 4, FALL, 1991, 555–94) points to the undermining of full-time employment.

7. Mingione, Enzo *Fragmented Societies: A Sociology of Economic Life beyond the Market Paradigm*, Oxford: Basil Blackwell, 1991, p. 4.

8. Laclau, Ernest *Politics and Ideology in Marxist Theory*, London: New Left Books, 1977, p. 157.

9. Robins, Kevin 'Prisoners of the City: whatever could a postmodern city be?', *New Formations*, 15, Winter, 1991, p. 18.

10. See Young, C., M. Petty, & A. Faulkner, *Education and Employment of Turkish and Lebanese Youth*, Canberra: Commonwealth Department of Education, Australian Government Publishing Service, 1980.

11. The term refugees will be used hereafter to distinguish these migrants from earlier Lebanese migrants because of the specific circumstances under which they left Lebanon and their heavy social and economic dependence on family and community support.

12. The problems faced by the Lebanese refugees and the inability of the communities to cope with the economic a welfare problems they faced actually forced it to develop a much more comprehensive refugee review and settlement policy. Hence when the Indo-Chinese refugees began arriving in 1978 there were state financial resources and services established to help them.

13. Cf. pp. 138–9 for the political significance of this event.

14. The terms cultural and social capital are derived from Bourdieu's usage. As Bourdieu outlines in *Distinction:* .
'The primary differences, those which distinguish the major classes of existence, derive from the overall volume of capital, understood as the set of actually usable resources and powers–economic capital, cultural capital, and also social capital. The distribution of the different classes (and class fractions thus runs from those who are best provided with both economic and cultural capital to those who are most deprived in both respects' Bourdieu op. cit. 1986, p. 114. Christian Joppke seeks to clarify Bourdieu's use of these terms in 'The Cultural Dimensions of Class Formation and Class Struggle: On the Social Theory of Pierre Bourdieu' *Berkeley Journal of Sociology*, XXXI, 1986, pp. 53–78. Cultural capital '... refers to cultural knowledge as a resource of power used by individuals and social groups to improve their positions within the social class structure'. (Joppke, p. 57). These he divides into institutionalised and incorporated capital referring to the official process of accreditation (e.g. educational degrees) and the

intergenerational transfer of knowledge. Social capital refers to '... the membership in social groups and the profits that can be appropriated by the strategic use of social relations in order to improve one's position'. (Joppke, pp. 59–60).

15. There have been a variety of official terms used to describe migrants to Australia. An older term was 'New Australians'. 'Non-English Speaking'(NES) represents an attempt to devise neutral acronyms to describe a general characteristic. However it was also widely adopted as a sociologically descriptive term to refer to the most disadvantaged migrant groups – those who lack the necessary cultural capital to secure good jobs and become socially mobile. Lack of English is equated with disadvantage, being working class and without portable middle class attributes.

16. The story of Lebanese as hawkers and peddlars is a central in early Lebanese settlement in the Americas, Australia and New Zealand. See Antonio Cecín *Los Libaneses en el Uruguay,* Montevideo, 1989, Alixa Naff *Becoming American: the Early Arab American Experience,* Carbondale & Edwardsville: Southern Illinois Press, 1985; A. Batrouney & T. Batrouney *The Lebanese in Australia,* Melbourne: A. E. Press, 1985; E. Valverde 'Integration and Identity in Argentina: the Lebanese in Tucuman' in A. Hourani & N. Shehadi (eds) *Lebanese in the World: A Century of Emigration*, London: I. B. Tauris, 1992.

17. See Table 2.1: Lebanese-Born population in Australia: 1911 to 1986.

18. This change of policy on emigration from Ottoman rule came after the massacres between Maronite and Druze populations on Mt Lebanon and European intervention in Ottoman affairs.

19. Safa, Elie *L'emigration libanaise,* Beirut 1960, pp. 188–91.

20. See Dubar, C. & S. Nasir *Les Classes Sociales au Liban*, Paris: Presses de la Foundation Nationale des Sciences Politiques, 1976 on emigration from Lebanon during 1900–1914 period and the volume of remittance inflow.

21. Khuri, Fuad 'The African-Lebanese Mulattoes of West Africa: a racial frontier' *The Anthropological Quarterly*, 2: 90–101, 1968.

22. For example Nick Shehadi a member of the national Rugby Union team and Head of SBS Television (a multilingual television station, Nick Aboud headed a national transport carrier TNT, David Malouf a prominent

Australian writer, Mansour a prominent clothing retailer, and Alec Alam a Senator in New South Wales politics.

23. Price, Charles 'Lebanese in Australia', unpub. paper, Department of Demography, Australian National University. Nov. 1983, Table 1: Persons Born in Arabic Countries and Table 2: Religions of Persons Born in Lebanon.

24. Estimate based on Price 1983 Table 2: Religious Persons Born in Lebanon.

25. Derived from 'Lebanese-Born population of Australia: Censuses 1911–1986', *Community Profiles: Lebanon Born*, Bureau of Immigration Research, Canberra: Australian Government Publishing Service, 1990, p. iv. and current immigrations statistics. Note that as occurred in the census and immigration records of North and South American states the Lebanese and Syrians were generally not differentiated until after independence in 1943. In the Australian case they were first differentiated in the 1954 census.

26. The Lebanese represent around 1.7% of the overseas born population. The largest groups are from the UK & Ireland 34.7%; Italy 8.1%; New Zealand 6.5%; Greece 4.2%; Germany 3.5%; Netherlands; Vietnam 2.6%; and Poland 2.1%.

27. *Community Profiles: Lebanon Born*, Bureau of Immigration Research, Table 2. Major Cities, Canberra: Australian Government Publishing Service, 1990, p. 4.

28. Kheir, Majid *Profile of the Lebanese Muslim Community*, Lebanese Muslim Association, Sydney, 1991, p. 4.

29. Ann Smith and Gintis Kaminskas 'Female Filipino Migration to Australia: an Overview', *Asian Migrant*, 5(3): 72–81, Table 1, p. 73.

30. Khuri, Fuad 'Parallel-Marriage Cousin marriage reconsidered: a Middle Eastern practice that nullifies the effects of marriage on the intensity of family relationships', *Man*, 5: 97–618, 1970; Peters, E. L. 'Aspects of Rank and Status among Muslims in a Lebanese village', in *Mediterranean Countrymen*, (ed.) J. Pitt-Rivers, pp. 159–202. Paris: Mouton, 1963.

31. Price op. cit., 1983, Table 4, 'Sex Ratios of Mediterranean Immigrants'.

32. Mingione op. cit., 1991, p. 152.

33. Ibid., p. 190.

34. See Davis, John *People of the Mediterranean: An Essay in Comparative Social Anthropology*, London: Routledge & Kegan Paul, 1977, p. 145.

35. Humphrey, Michael, *Family, Work and Unemployment: Lebanese Settlement in Sydney*, Canberra: Australian Government Publishing Service, 1984, pp. 40–1.

36. Khuri, Fuad *From Village to Suburb: Order and Change in Greater Beirut*, Chicago: University of Chicago, 1975.

37. Harvey, David *The Urban Experience*, Oxford: Basil Blackwell, 1989, p. 266.

38. Ibid., p. 32.

39. Ibid., p. 120.

40. Portes, Alejandro & Julia Sensenbrenner 'Embeddedness and Immigration: Notes on the Social Determinants of Economic Action' *American Journal of Sociology*, 98(6), 1320–50, 1993, p. 331.

41. The pattern of distribution varies with ethnic group. While the Lebanese were concentrated in Sydney the Turks and Greeks were concentrated in Melbourne. See *Profile 81*, 1981 Census Data on Persons Born in Lebanon, Department of Immigration & Ethnic Affairs, Canberra: AGPS 1984. By 1986 almost three-quarters (74.6%) of the Lebanese born population lived in Australia and nearly all of these 97.6% lived in Sydney. (Community Profiles Lebanese Born, 1990, Table 1. Comparison between 1981 & 1986 Censuses.)

42. There are a variety of sources on these organisations which are all based on self reporting. The most comprehensive are the Arabic Resource Directories (1983, 1985) compiled by the Lebanese Settlement Council created by the Department of Immigration and Ethnic Affairs.

43. Cf. pp. 63–4.

44. Nabti, Patricia 'Emigration from a Lebanese Village: A Case Study of Bishmizzine', in A. Hourani & N. Shehadi (eds) *Lebanese in the World: A Century of Emigration*, London: I. B. Tauris, 1992, pp. 41–63, p. 60.

45. Discussion on migration in the Balkans from the 19th century also provides evidence of the way emigration from remote communities can actually preserve the autonomy of regions rather than undermine them. Islamoglu-Inan, H. (ed.) *The Ottoman Economy in the World Economy*, Cambridge: Cambridge U. P., 1987.

46. Bourdieu, Pierre 'The Social Space and the Genesis of Groups',

Theory and Society, 14, 723–744, 1985, p. 741.

47. See Humphrey, Michael 'Community, Mosque and Ethnic Politics', *Australian and New Zealand Journal of Sociology*, XXIII: 233–45, 1988.

48. Humphrey, Michael 'Islam, Sect and State: the Lebanese Case', Papers on Lebanon, No. 11, Centre for Lebanese Studies, Oxford, 1989.

49. See 'The Council of the Municipality of Canterbury v. The Moslem Alawy Society Ltd.' in the High Court of Australia, Sydney Office of the Registry No. 33 of 1985.

50. Humphrey, Michael, 'Is this a Mosque Free-Zone?', *Migration Action*, No. 12, pp. 12–17, 1989. p. 12.

51. Cf. Kepel, Gilles *Les Banlieues de l'Islam*, Paris: Editions du Seuil, 1987; Nielsen, Jorge *Muslims in Western Europe*, Edinburgh: Edinburgh University Press, 1992.

52. Their Maronite Catholicism was eclipsed by the Australian-Irish Catholic institutions in Australia. The role of churches in incorporating different Catholic ethnic minorities is a central theme in McKay's work on third generation Lebanese in Australia. McKay, Jim *Phoenician Farewell: Third Generation Lebanese*, Melbourne: Ashwood House Academic,1989.

53. Humphrey op. cit. 1988.

54. Khuri op. cit., 1975, p. 169–70.

55. Table 3.2: Eligibility category of settler arrivals, Australia, 1982–3 & 1991–2, *Australian Population Trends and Prospects, 1992*. Bureau of Immigration Research, Canberra: Australian Government Publishing Service, 1992.

56. Jasso, Guillermina & Mark R. Rosenzweig *The Chosen People: Immigranst in the United States*, New York: Russell Sage Foundation, 1990, Table 1.4.

57. Cf. p. 23, n. 17.

58. McKay op. cit., 1989, pp. 43–4.

59. Collins, Jock *Migrant Hands in a Distant Land: Australia's post-war immigration*, Sydney & London: Pluto Press, 1988, p. 89.

60. Ibid., p. 81.

61. Humphrey Michael op. cit., Canberra: AGPS, 1984, p. 70.

62. Humphrey op. cit., 1984, p. 69.

63. Ibid., p. 70. 61% of male and 74% of female unemployed had been employed in factory or labouring jobs.

64. Mingione op. cit., 1991, p. 189.

65. S. Castles, J. Collins, K. Gibson, D. Tait and C. Alcorso *The Global Milkbar and the Local Sweatshop: Ethnic Small Business and the Economic Restructuring of Sydney*, Centre for Multicultural Studies, University of Wollongong, 1991, p. 24.

66. Williams, A. J. Small Business Failures in Australia: a Longitudinal Study' Unpub. Paper. The University of Newcastle, 1982. In a longitudinal study over eight years (1973–81) he found that 91.1% of the small businesses started in 1973 failed. He found the greatest failure rate in the first two years of operation (43.5%).

67. Humphrey, Michael op. cit., Table 6.4, p. 50.

68. Khuri op. cit., 1975, p. 117.

69. Humphrey op. cit., 1984, Table 8.9, p. 77.

70. The Maintenance Guarantee provision allows the migration of relatives whose financial position has been underwritten by other family members in Australia. While it denies people the right to a pension it does not exclude them from collecting unemployment benefits. In an attempt to reduce welfare expenditure on unemployment benefits the Department of Social Security decided to declare a large number of people in this situation unemployable thereby denying them unemployment benefits.

71. Phizacklea, Annie 'Entrepreneurship, Ethnicity and Gender' in Sallie Westwood & Parminder Bhachu (eds) *Enterprising Women: Ethnicity Economy and Gender Relations*, London: Routledge, 1987, p. 27.

72. Humphrey op. cit., 1984 Table 5.3, p. 41.

73. Ibid., Table 6.6, p. 52.

74. Offe, Claus *Disorganised Capitalism, Contemporary Transformations of Work and Politics*, Cambridge: Polity Press, 1985, p. 48.

75. Ibid., p. 48.

Chapter Three

1. Longrigg, Stephen *Syria and Lebanon Under the French Mandate*, Oxford: Oxford University Press, 1958, p. 117.

2. Ladas, Stephen *The Exchange of Minorities: Bulgaria, Greece and Turkey*, New York: Macmillan, 1932, p. 724.

3. Lozios, Peter 'Intercommunal Killing in Cyprus' *Man*, 23(4), 1988: 639–53, p. 643.

4. Lonrigg op. cit., 1958, p. 21.

5. Fisk, Robert *Pity the Nation: Lebanon at War*, Oxford: Oxford University Press, 1991, p. 63.

6. Jansen, G. H. *Militant Islam*, London: Pan Books, 1979, p. 66.

7. Dib, George 'Selections from Riadh Solh's Speech in the Assembly (7 Oct. 1943), embodying the Main Principles of the Lebanese National Pact', *Middle East Forum* 34, Jan., 1959.

8. Salibi, Kamal *A House of Many Mansions: Tthe History of Lebanon Reconsidered*, London: I. B. Tauris, 1988, p. 186; el-Khazen, Farid 'The Communal Pact of National Identities' Papers on Lebanon No. 12, Centre for Lebanese Studies, Oxford, 1991, p. 39. Hudson, Michael *The Precarious Republic: political modernisation in Lebanon*, New York: Random House, 1968.

10. Heiberg, M. *Making of the Basque Nation*, Cambridge: Cambridge U. P. 1989, p. 240.

11. In 1920 when the French received the Mandate they found a developed primary and secondary school system which included American, British, and French Missionary schools as well as a number of state primary schools which had been established under Ottoman rule. See Jansen op. cit., 1979, p. 71.

12. Ibid., p. 24.

13. Burke III, Edmund 'Rural Collective Action and the Emergence of Modern Lebanon' in N. Shehadi & Dana Haffar Mills (eds) *Lebanon: a History of Conflict and Consensus*, London: I. B. Tauris, 1988, p. 19.

14. Saba, Paul 'The Creation of the Lebanese Economy: Economic Growth in the Nineteenth and Early Twentieth Centuries'. In *Essays on the Crisis in Lebanon*, ed. Roger Owen, pp. 1–22. London: Ithaca Press, 1976 and Owen, Roger 'The Political Economy of Grand Liban 1920–1970' In Owen op. cit.,1976.

15. Longrigg op. cit., 1958, p. 33. 16. Ibid., p. 284.

16. Ibid., p. 284.

17. Buheiry, Marwan 'Beirut's Role in the Political Economy of the French Mandate 1919–39', Papers on Lebanon No. 4, Centre for Lebanese Studies, Oxford, 1986.

18. Hashimoto, Kohei 'Lebanese Population Movement: 1920–39' in A. Hourani & N. Shehadi (eds) op. cit., 1993.

19. Buheiry op. cit., 1986, p. 11.

20. Ibid., p. 21.

21. Hudson op. cit., 1968.

22. Harvey, 1989 op. cit., p. 265.

23. Ibid., p. 265.

24. Ibid., p. 266.

25. Farsoun, Karen & S. Farsoun, 'Class Patterns of Association Among Kinsmen in Contemporary Lebanon', Anthropology Quarterly, 47(1), 1974.

26. Ibid., p. 116.

27. Ibid., p. 118.

28. Sayigh, Yusuf *Entrepreneurs in Lebanon*, Cambridge: Harvard University Press, 1962 found that of 3,492 establishments registered at the Beirut Chamber of Commerce 2,160 were single ownership, 1,230 were partnerships, and 102 were corporations.

29. Cooke, Miriam 'Women Write War', *Papers on Lebanon*, No. 6, Centre for Lebanese Studies, Oxford, July, 1987, p. 14.

30. Even amongst Lebanese emigrants these village attachments are reinforced when they register the birth of their children to secure Lebanese nationality. Their registration is recorded in the register of the village, not simply a national register.

31. Joseph, Suad 'The Family as Security and Bondage in Lebanon' in H. Safa (ed.) *Towards a Political Economy of Urbanisation in Third World Countries*, Delhi: Oxford University Press 1982, p. 166.

32. Ibid., p. 166.

33. Ibid., p. 155.

34. 'The Lebanese Law Wears a Moustache', *Monday Morning*, 24 February 1975, Beirut.

35. Gilsenan, Michael *Recognizing Islam: an Anthropologist's Introduction*, London: Croom Helm, 1982, pp. 95–115.

36. Ibid., p. 110.

37. Khuri, Fuad *Imams and Emirs: State, Religion and Sects in Islam*, London: Saqi Books, 1990, p. 168.

38. Ibid., p. 173.

39. Johnson, Michael 'Factional Politics in Lebanon: The Case of the 'Islamic Society of Benevolent Intentions' (Al Maqasid) in Beirut' Middle East Studies, 14(1), 56–75, 1978, pp. 62–3.

40. Cooke op. cit., 1987, p. 12.

41. Johnson, Michael *Class and Client in Beirut: The Sunni Muslim Community and the Lebanese State 1840–1985*, London: Ithaca Press, 1986, p. 213.

42. Humphrey, Michael op. cit., 1989.

43. Johnson op. cit., 1986, p. 213.

44. Cooke op. cit., 1987.

Chapter Four

1. Bourdieu, Pierre *The Outline of Theory and Practice*, Cambridge: Cambridge University Press, 1977, p. 190.

2. Bourdieu, Pierre *Algeria 1960*, London: Cambridge University Press, 1979, p. 70.

3 Woollacott, Martin 'The high political cost of morality campaigns', *Sydney Morning Herald*, 24th Jan 1994, p. 9.

4. Abel, Richard L. 'A Comparative Theory of Disputes and Law'. *Law and Society Review*, 8, 1973, p. 217.

5. Foucault, M. 'Power and Norm: Notes', in *Michel Foucault: Power, Truth, Strategy*, (eds) M. Morris & P. Patton, (eds) Sydney: Feral Publications. 1979, p. 64.

6. Bourdieu op. cit., 1977, p. 40.

7. Bruner, Jerome 'The Narrative Construction of Reality' *Critical Inquiry*, Autumn, 1991, 1–21, p. 18.

8. Gilsenan, Michael 'Lying, Honour and Contradiction'. In *Transactions & Meaning*, ed. B. Kapferer, Philadelphia: Institute for the Study of Human Relations, 1976.

9. Bourdieu op. cit., 1977, p. 22.

10. Massell, Gregory *The Surrogate Proletariat: Moslem Women and Revolutionary Struggles in Soviet Central Asia, 1919–1929*, New Jersey: Princeton U. P. 1974, p. 410.

11. Ibid., p. 401.

12. Here *Shari'a* Law is used in its restricted sense to refer to the actual legal provisions of Islamic Law incorporated as law in the Sunni and Shi'i Muslim personal laws in Lebanon.

13. Bourdieu employs 'necessity' as a class concept which makes a virtue of wanting only what is appropriate to one's identity and perception of social trajectory. Bourdieu, Pierre *Distinction: A Critique of the Judgement of Taste*, London: Routledge & Kegan Paul, 1984, pp. 371–4.

14. In 1989 three Muslim high school students in Creil were banned from wearing a head scarf on the grounds that it transgressed the secularism of French state schools. The issue has yet to be definitely decided. Solé, Robert 'Lifting a veil of fear from French schools', *Guardian Weekly*, 25 September, 1994, p. 14.

15. Ahmed, Leila *Women and Gender in Islam*, New Haven: Yale U. P. 1992.

16. Kirby, Vicki 'On the cutting edge: feminism and clitoridectomy', *Australian Feminist Studies*, 5: 35–55, 1987.

17. 'Court monitors circumcised girls', *The Sydney Morning Herald*, 1 March, 1994, p. 2.

18. Walker, Alice *Possessing the Secret of Joy*, New York: Harcourt Brace Jovanovich, 1992.

19. The minimum age of marriage was increased from 16 to 18 years as a result of a recommendation of the Australian Law Reform Commission report, '*Multiculturalism and the Law*', Canberra: AGPS, 1993.

20. Under the Marriage Act 1961–73 Part II, sections 11 & 12, the marriageable age for minors is 18 years for boys and girls 16 years for minors. However a boy who has attained the age of 16 years and a girl who has attained the age of 14 years can apply to a judge or magistrate for an order authorising him or her to marry a particular person of marriageable age. A judge or magistrate may grant permission to marry in exceptional or unusual circumstances. In practice the minimum age at which magistrates in Sydney permit the marriage of girls was, until a recent change of law, 15 years.

21. Cohabitation and consummation do not necessarily immediately follow the signing of the marriage contract. Marriage between Muslims passes through three distinct stages; engagement, the signing of the contract (*al khitab*) and consummation. Although in legal terms they may be

shortened to one ceremony, the signing of the contract, custom generally enforces the observance of the others. The length of time between the marriage ceremony and the consummation may vary from almost immediately to up until a year or more.

22. *'Asl* refers to the social ranking of family in the context of community. It is regarded as an attribute which inheres in an individual by descent. In migration the social order of family ranking in villages is frequently overturned and *'asl* undermined with respected families becoming impoverished and poor families succeeding financially.

23. de Costa, Caroline 'Pregnancy Outcomes in Lebanese-born Women in Western Sydney', *The Medical Journal of Australia*, v. 149, pp. 457–60, 7 November 1988.

24. Bourdieu, Pierre *The Outline of Theory and Practice*, Cambridge: Cambridge University Press, 1977, p. 57.

25. Ibid., p. 58.

26. de Costa revealed that almost 80% of women did not book into hospitals until very late – after the 29th week of pregnancy. Around 40% booked in after the 32nd week. This led to greater complications during the pregnancy and childbirth including almost twice the rate of miscarriage and very low rates of cervical smear-tests. de Costa op. cit., 1988, p. 457.

27. Bourdieu, Pierre *Algeria 1960*, Cambridge: Cambridge U. P., 1979, p. 20.

28. Rosen, Lawrence 'Equity and Discretion in a Modern Islamic Legal System, *Law and Society Review*, 15: 217–45, 1981, p. 224.

29. During a visit to Lebanon in 1979–80 I was asked by a sheik in Sydney to deliver some letters to a Shari'a Court judge in Beirut. These letters sought advice and points of legal clarification on custody and divorce matters.

30. In Islamic law the right to divorce belongs almost exclusively to the husband. Other forms of divorce are where the husband's right of repudiation is either suspended or delegated. The former can occur, for example, in the event of a husband marrying a second wife. The latter can occur where a husband has conferred on the wife the power to repudiate herself (*talaqi-tafwid*). Another possible form of divorce is *khul'*, divorce by mutual agreement. Usually the wife will offer to pay a certain sum in return for the agreement of the husband to release her from the marriage

tie.

31. Multiculturalism and the Law, Australian Law Reform Commission, 1993.

32. Hewett, Tony 'Muslims: law must recognise dower', *Sydney Morning Herald*, 25 September, 1991, p. 11; and 'Our laws upset love and marriage, Islam-style' *Sydney Morning Herald*, 26 September, 1991.

Chapter Five

1. Harvey op. cit., 1989, p. 249.

2. There are several terms Lebanese use to refer to honour, *sharaf*, *'ird*, and *sum'a*. *Sharaf* is a general term which refers to a family's or individual's standing in the community and is connected with other concepts such as *'asl* meaning of good breeding or stock. *'Ird* relates to honour which men have invested in the women of the family. It is usually referred to as sexual modesty. As Khuri states: 'Being the *'ird* of men, women (wife–mother, sister–daughter) have no *'ird* of their own. ' Khuri op. cit., 1970, p. 614. The *suma'a* is most often alluded to in conversation by Lebanese and has the meaning of reputation. A man's *sum'a* is assessed by his public acts and relate to the way he fulfils his family obligations, his participation in community affairs and his readiness to mediate in disputes. He is always on guard against insults to his *'ird*.

3. Local institutions are the major focus in most studies of Muslim immigrant communities in Western Europe. See Etienne, Bruno *La France et l'Islam*, Paris: Hachette, 1989; Gerholm, Tomas & Lithman, Yngve Georg *The New Islamic Presence in Western Europe*, London: Mansell Publishing Limited, 1988; Kepel, Gilles *les Banlieues de l'Islam*, Paris: Editions du Seuil, 1987; Nielsen, Jorge *Muslims in Western Europe*, Edinburgh: Edinburgh University Press, 1992.

4. The *Amicale des Algériens in France*, for example, has functioned as a political linking the FLN structures in Algeria with the communist linked trade union federation, the CGT. See Nielsen op. cit., 1992, p. 16.

5. In fact the Lebanese in general had gained the reputation for being a violent group amongst the magistracy. One magistrate, while passing

sentence on a Lebanese convicted of an assault charge, came under considerable public criticism for the comment that 'Lebanese should not carry knives'.

6. A similar concept, 'idiotes', exists in Greek culture, 'idiotes'. Disregard of one's social context, especially acting without support or not considering the consequences of one's action, is the mark of a stupid man. Davis, John *People of the Mediterranean: An Essay in Comparative Social Anthropology*, London: Routledge & Kegan Paul, 1977.

7. Use of the courtroom to publicly take revenge in Lebanon is very common (correspondence with Michael Gilsenan).

8. Haj v. Minister for Immigration & Ethnic Affairs, In the Federal Court of Australia, NSW District Registry, General Division. Transcript No. G. 68 of 1981.

9. The Syrian Socialist Nationalist Party, also known as the Partie Populaire Syrienne (PPS), advocates a non-sectarian socialist state of Greater Syria which incorporates Lebanon. Its success in recruiting Arab immigrants in Sydney only rivals that of the Lebanese World Cultural Union, a Maronite organisation founded in the early 1920s by Lebanese American immigrants to promote the maintenance of a distinctive Lebanese culture amongst immigrant communities. For a history and ideological study of the SSNP see Zuwiyya-Yamak, L. *The Syrian Social National Party*, Cambridge: Harvard University Press, 1966.

10. This incident was widely publicised at the time in the Arabic, and Australian press and represented an effective lobbying of public opinion against the growing threat of 'Arab terrorism' in Australia. For example 'Iraq–Iran war leads to local Arab violence', *The Bulletin*, Tuesday 11 November 1980 and 'Gulf war comes to Sydney suburbs', *The Sydney Morning Herald*, Tuesday, 11 November 1980.

11. There still remains a split amongst Greek immigrant communities in Australia over the acceptance of the Greek Orthodox Church and Archbishop. There are congregations which are regarded as in or the group of priests who were originally recruited by village communities.

12. The principal benefactors of the Imam Ali (Lakemba) mosque were Saudi Arabia ($300,000), Kuwait ($80,000) and Libya ($90,000). The balance was raised locally. See 'Islamic world keeps an eye on Australian Moslems' in *The Financial Review*, Wednesday, 5 March 1980.

13. The designation 'Imam' refers to the one who leads Friday prayer. 'Shaikh' is a term attributing religious learning.

14. One Lebanese Shi'a shaikh who had obtained permission to undertake religious work in Australia through the Australian Embassy in Iran was actually held in custody overnight when he first arrived at Sydney airport. His religious robes, turban and the Iranian embarkation stamp in his passport so alarmed Immigration officials that he was kept in detention until his status was clarified the next day. The large Lebanese Shi'i reception committee at the airport was extremely angry at such disrespectful treatment of their shaikh.

15. See Humphrey, Michael op. cit., 1989 and 'Mosque, Community and Ethnic Politics' in the *Australian and New Zealand Journal of Sociology*, July, 23(2): 233–45, 1987.

16. One such photograph showing sectarian leaders and the Australian Prime Minister Bob Hawke was even published in another Maronite diaspora newspaper in Paris, *Revue Libanais, 1989.*

17. Alison, Col 'Arab Australians in hostage mission' *The Sydney Morning Herald*, Friday, 16 November 1990, p. 9.

18. Yarwood, A. T. *Asian Migration to Australia; The Background to Exclusion, 1896–23*, Parkville: Melbourne University Press 1964, p. 141.

19. Mackay op. cit., 1990, p. 120.

20. Australian Lebanese Committee, Official Programme, 18th–20th September, 1981.

21. See 'Praying Worker Loses Job' *The Sydney Morning Herald*, Friday, April 17, 1981.

22. Personal interviews with primary school teachers from schools with large Muslim populations.

23. Despite the advice of a visiting adviser on Muslim Minorities to the Government of Saudi Arabia and a note in the 'Islamic Council of NSW President's Annual Report 1981–82' indicating it had recommended that member societies delete all names that suggested ethnic, national or religious affiliation many members retain affiliation in their titles; e.g. the Lebanese Muslim Association, Muslim Alawy Society, Albanian Muslim Society and the Turkish Society of Victoria.

24. Amongst the Sunni mosque community the former Australian Prime Minister Gough Whitlam, for example, is highly regarded because of his

status and sympathy for the plight of the Palestinians not because of respect or knowledge of his Labour government's achievements.

25. Fischer, Michael M. J. & Mehdi Abedi *Debating Muslims; Cultural Dialogues in Postmodernity and Tradition*, Wisconsin: University of Wisconsin Press, 1990, p. 338.

26. Ibid., p. 337.

27. Rieff, David *Los Angeles: Capital of the Third World*, London: Phoenix, 1993, p. 45.

Chapter Six

1. Rieff op. cit., 1993, p. 194.
2. Ibid., p. 146.
3. Harvey op. cit., 1989, p. 151.
4. It was recently reported by the Lebanese Ministry of the Interior that Australia was the primary target of Lebanese drug exports. Most, it was claimed, was carried in small quantities (3kg to 5kg) by individual travellers. Obeid, Maha 'Australia the main target for Lebanese drug exports', *The Australian*, Tuesday 29 March 1994, p. 10.
5. Stewart, Cameron & Richard Jinman 'Violence tarnishes Macedonians; Bolkus', *The Australia*, 12 April 1994, p. 4.
6. Humphrey, Michael 'Sectarianism and the Politics of Identity: the Lebanese in Sydney', in A. Hourani & N. Shehadi (eds) *Lebanese in the World: A Century of Emigration*, London: I. B. Tauris, 1993, pp. 443–71.
7. Spivak, Gayatri Chakravorty *The Post-Colonial Critic: Interviews, Strategies, Dialogues*, Ed. Sarah Harasym, New York & London: Routledge, 1990, p. 61.
8. Shaikh Chami, the Lebanese Sunni shaikh reported one of his early activities was to import Qur'ans to make people aware of their religion. Poor literacy in Arabic and concern about the religious offence caused by mispronunciation of the Sacred Book meant that he also imported English translations.
9. Horton cited in Basil Davidson *The Black Man's Burden: Africa and the Curse of the Nation-State*, New York: Random House, 1992, p. 39.
10. Ahmed, Leila *Women and Gender in Islam*, New Haven: Yale U. P.

1992.

11. Humphrey, Michael *Family, Work and Unemployment: Lebanese settlement in Sydney*, Canberra: Australian Government Publishing Service, 1984.

12. Nielson op. cit., 1992.

13. Humphrey, Michael 'Ethnic History, Nationalism and Transnationalism: Argentine Arab and Jewish Cultures' in *Immigrants and Minorities*, 1998 (forthcoming) and Estela Valverde 'The Lebanese in Túcuman' in N. Shehadi & A. Hourani (eds) *Lebanese in the World: a Century of Lebanese Emigration*, London: I. B. Tauris, 1993.

14. LEBNET is a daily electronic bulletin sent from Colombia University in the United States on the INTERNET computer communications network which is available free, on request, to anyone with an electronic mail address.

15. Videoing functions can have a very dampening effect because everyone becomes acutely aware their behaviour is under scrutiny by a potentially very large audience, in Sydney, Lebanon and other parts of the diaspora. On one occasion at a Sunni Muslim wedding the younger brother of the groom was very anxious to show the video to his father. He wanted to consult him about the suitability of one girl who had been videoed as a potential wife. He had not dared to approach her in the context of the filmed event.

16. Abaza, Mona & Georg Stauth 'Occidental Reason, Orientalism, Islamic Fundamentalism: A Critique' in M. Albrow & Elizabeth King (eds) *Globalisation, Knowledge and Society*, London: Sage Publications, 1990, pp. 209–30.

17. One example of this legal approval is the document 'Guidelines to Current Burial Procedures in NSW Australia with Janazaah Supplement' (1984) produced in co-operation with the Islamic Burial Trust, The Funeral & Allied Industries Union of NSW, The Dignified Funerals (Five Dock) Pty. Ltd. of Lakemba and the Rockwood Cemetery. The document was produced only after a long battle with Unions and the Anglican Church about Muslim burial on consecrated Anglican ground. Rookwood is the largest cemetery in Australia. In Sydney idiom to be 'As crook as Rookwood' means to be 'dead on your feet'!

18. Cf. pp. 144–5.

19. Fischer & Abedi op. cit., 1990, p. 288.

Bibliography

Abel, Richard L. 'A Comparative Theory of Disputes and Law'. *Law and Society Review*, 8, 1973.

Barbalet, J. M. *Citizenship: Rights, Struggle and Class Inequality*, Milton Keynes: Open University Press 1988, p. 2.

Batrouney, A. & T. Batrouney *The Lebanese in Australia*, Melbourne: A. E. Press, 1985.

Bourdieu, Pierre *The Outline of Theory and Practice*, Cambridge: Cambridge University Press, 1977, p. 40.

—*Distinction: A Social Critique of the Judgement of Taste*, London: Routledge Kegan Paul,1984.

—'The Social Space and the Genesis of Groups' *Theory and Society*, 14: 723–44, 1985.

Broad, David 'Global Economic Restructuring and the Casualisation of Work in the Center: With Canadian Illustrations', *Review*, XIV, 4, Fall 1991, 555–94.

Bruner, Jerome 'The Narrative Construction of Reality' *Critical Inquiry*, Autumn, 1991, 1–21, p. 18.

Buheiry, Marwan 'Beirut's Role in the Political Economy of the French Mandate 1919–39', Papers on Lebanon No. 4, Centre for Lebanese Studies, Oxford, 1986.

Burke III, Edmund 'Rural Collective Action and the Emergence of Modern Lebanon' in N. Shehadi & Dana Haffar Mills (eds) *Lebanon: a History of Conflict and Consensus*, London: I. B. Tauris, 1988.

Castles, S. J. Collins, K. Gibson, D. Tait & C. Alcorso *The Global Milkbar and the Local Sweatshop: Ethnic Small Business and the Economic Restructuring of Sydney*, Centre for Multicultural Studies, University of Wollongong, 1991.

Cecín, Antonio *Los Libaneses en el Uruguay*, Montevideo, 1989.

Collins, Jock *Migrant Hands in a Distant Land: Australia's Post-war Immigration*, Sydney & London: Pluto Press, 1988.

Cooke, Miriam, 'Women Write War' *Papers on Lebanon, No. 6*, Centre for Lebanese Studies, Oxford, July, 1987.

Davis, John *People of the Mediterranean: An Essay in Comparative Social Anthropology*, London: Routledge & Kegan Paul, 1977.

de Costa, Caroline 'Pregnancy Outcomes in Lebanese-born Women in Western Sydney', *The Medical Journal of Australia*, v. 149, pp. 457–60, Nov. 7, 1988.

Dib, George 'Selections from Riadh Solh's Speech in the Assembly (7 Oct. 1943), embodying the Main Principles of the Lebanese National Pact', *Middle East Forum* 34, Jan. 1959.

Dubar, C. & S. Nasir *Les classes sociales au Liban*, Paris: Presses de la Foundation Nationale des Sciences Politiques, 1976.

Etienne, Bruno *La France et l'islam*, Paris: Hachette, 1989.

Farsoun, Karen & S. Farsoun 'Class Patterns of Association Among Kinsmen in Contemporary Lebanon', *Anthropology Quarterly*, 47(1), 1974.

Fischer, Michael M. J. and Mehdi Abedi *Debating Muslims: Cultural Dialogues in Postmodernity and Tradition*, Wisconsin: University of Wisconsin Press, 1990.

Foucault, M. 'Power and Norm: Notes', in *Michel Foucault: Power, Truth, Strategy*, M. Morris & P. Patton (eds), Sydney: Feral Publications, 1979.

Gerholm, Tomas & Yngve Georg Lithman *The New Islamic Presence in Western Europe*, London: Mansell Publishing Limited, 1988.

Gilsenan, Michael 'Lying, Honour and Contradiction'. In *Transactions & Meaning*, ed. B. Kapferer, Philadelphia: Institute for the Study of Human Relations, 1976.

—*Recognizing Islam: an Anthropologists Introduction*, London: Croom Helm, 1982.

Harvey, David *The Urban Experience*, Oxford: Basil Blackwell, 1989.

Hashimoto, Kohei 'Lebanese Population Movement: 1920–39' in A. Hourani & N. Shehadi (eds) *Lebanese in the World*, London: I. B. Tauris, 1993.

Heiberg, Marianne *Making of the Basque Nation*, Cambridge: Cambridge

U. P. 1989.

Hudson, Michael *The Precarious Republic: Political Modernisation in Lebanon*, New York: Random House, 1968.

Humphrey, Michael *Family, Work and Unemployment: Lebanese Settlement in Sydney*, Canberra: Australian Government Publishing Service, 1984, pp. 40–1.

—'Community, Mosque and Ethnic Politics', *Australian and New Zealand Journal of Sociology*, XXIII: 233–45, 1988.

—'Is this a Mosque Free-Zone? Islam and the State in Australia', *Migration Action*, January, No. 12,pp. 12–17, 1989.

—'Islam, Sect and State: the Lebanese Case', Centre for Lebanese Studies, Occasional Paper, No. 11, July, 1989.

—'Sectarianism and the Politics of Identity: the Lebanese in Sydney', in A. Hourani & N. Shehadi (eds) *Lebanese in the World: A Century of Emigration*, London: I. B. Tauris, 1993, pp. 443–71.

—'Ethnic History, Nationalism and Transnationalism: Argentine Arab and Jewish Cultures' *Immigrants and Minorities* 8, (forthcoming).

Jansen, G. H. *Militant Islam*, London: Pan Books,1979.

Jasso, Guillermina & Mark R. Rosenzweig *The Chosen People: Immigrants in the United States,* New York: Russell Sage Foundation, 1990.

Johnson, Michael 'Factional Politics in Lebanon: The Case of the "Islamic Society of Benevolent Intentions" (Al Maqasid) in Beirut' *Middle East Studies*, 14(1), 56–75, 1978.

—*Class and Client in Beirut: The Sunni Muslim Community and the Lebanese State 1840–1985*, London: Ithaca Press, 1986.

Joppke, Christian 'The Cultural Dimensions of Class Formation and Class Struggle: in the Social Theory of Pierre Bourdieu' *Berkeley Journal of Sociology*, XXXI, 1986, pp. 53–78.

Joseph, Suad 'The Family as Security and Bondage in Lebanon' in H. Safa (ed.) *Towards a Political Economy of Urbanisation in Third World Countries*, Dehli: Oxford U. P. 1982.

Kepel, Gilles *Les Banlieues de l'Islam,* Paris: Editions du Seuil, 1987.

Kheir, Majid *Profile of the Lebanese Muslim Community*, Lebanese Muslim Association, Sydney, 1991, p. 4.

Khuri, Fuad 'The African-Lebanese Mulattoes of West Africa: a racial frontier' *The Anthropological Quarterly*, 2: 90–101, 1968.

—'Parallel–Marriage Cousin Marriage Reconsidered: a Middle Eastern Practice that Nullifies the Effects of Marriage on the Intensity of Family Relationships', *Man*, 5: 97–618, 1970.

—*From Village to Suburb: Order and Change in Greater Beirut*, Chicago: University of Chicago, 1975.

—*Imams and Emirs: State, Religion and Sects in Islam*, London: Saqi Books, 1990, p. 168.

Kirby, Vicki 'On the Cutting Edge: Feminism and Clitorodectomy', *Australian Feminist Studies*, 5: 35–55, 1987.

Laclau, Ernest *Politics and Ideology in Marxist Theory*, London: New Left Books, 1977.

Ladas, Stephen *The Exchange of Minorities: Bulgaria, Greece and Turkey*, New York: Macmillan, 1932.

Lozios, Peter 'Intercommunal Killing in Cyprus' *Man*, 23(4), 1988: 639–53.

McKay, Jim *Phoenician Farewell: Third Generation Lebanese*, Melbourne: Ashwood House Academic, 1989.

Marshall, T. H. *Citizenship and Social Class and other Essays*, Cambridge: Cambridge University Press, 1950.

Massell, Gregory *The Surrogate Proletariat: Moslem Women and Revolutionary Struggles in Soviet Central Asia, 1919–1929*, New Jersey: Princeton U. P. 1974.

Mingione, Enzo *Fragmented Societies: A Sociology of Economic Life Beyond the Market Paradigm*, Oxford: Basil Blackwell, 1991.

Nabti, Patricia 'Emigration from a Lebanese Village: A Case Study of Bishmizzine', in A. Hourani & N. Shehadi (eds) *Lebanese in the World: A Century of Emigration*, London: I. B. Tauris, 1992, pp. 41–63.

Naff, Alixa *Becoming American: the Early Arab American Experience*, Carbondale & Edwardsville: Southern Illinois Press, 1985.

Nielsen, Jorgen *Muslims in Western Europe*, Edinburgh: Edinburgh University Press, 1992.

Offe, Claus *Disorganised Capitalism: Contemporary Transformations of Work and Politics*, Cambridge: Polity Press, 1985.

Owen, Roger 'The Political Economy of Grand Liban 1920–1970' In *Essays on the Crisis in Lebanon*, ed. Roger Owen, (pp. 23–32) London: Ithaca

Press, 1976.

Peters, E. L. 'Aspects of Rank and Status among Muslims in a Lebanese Village', in *Mediterranean Countrymen,* ed. J. Pitt-Rivers, pp. 159–202. Paris: Mouton, 1963.

Phizacklea, Annie 'Entrepreneurship, Ethnicity and Gender' in Sallie Westwood & Parminder Bhachu (eds) *Enterprising Women: Ethnicity Economy and Gender Relations,* London: Routledge, 1987.

Portes, Alejandro & Julia Sensenbrenner 'Embeddedness and Immigration: Notes on the Social Determinants of Economic Action' *American Journal of Sociology,* 98(6), 1320–50, 1993.

Price, Charles 'Lebanese in Australia', unpub. paper, Department of Demography, Australian National University. Nov. 1983.

Profile 81, 1981 Census Data on Persons Born in Lebanon, Department of Immigration & Ethnic Affairs, Canberra: AGPS 1984.

Rieff, David *Los Angeles: Capital of the Third World,* London: Phoenix, 1991.

Robins, Kevin 'Prisoners of the City: Whatever Could a Postmodern City Be?' *New Formations,* 15, Winter 1991.

Rosen, Lawrence 'Equity and Discretion in a Modern Islamic Legal System', *Law and Society Review,* 15: 217–45, 1981.

Saba, Paul 'The Creation of the Lebanese Economy: Economic Growth in the Nineteenth and Early Twentieth Centuries'. In *Essays on the Crisis in Lebanon,* ed. Roger Owen, pp. 1–22. London: Ithaca Press, 1976.

Sarmiento, Domingo *Civilizacion y Barbarie,* Buenos Aires: Felix Lajoune, 1889.

Sayigh, Yusuf *Entrepreneurs in Lebanon,* Cambridge: Harvard University Press, 1962.

Smith, Ann and Gintis Kaminskas 'Female Filipino Migration to Australia: an Overview', *Asian Migrant,* 5(3): 72–81.

Soja, Edward *Postmodern Geographies: the Reassertion of Space in Critical Social Theory,* London, New York: Verso, 1989.

Spivak, Gayatri Chakravorty *The Post-Colonial Critic: Interviews, Strategies, Dialogues,* ed. Sarah Harasym, New York & London: Routledge, 1990.

Valverde, E. 'Integration and Identity in Argentina: the Lebanese in Tucuman' in A. Hourani & N. Shehadi (eds) *Lebanese in the World: A Century of Emigration,* London: I. B. Tauris, 1992.

Walker, Alice *Possesing the Secret of Joy,* New York: Harcourt Brace

Jovanovich, 1992.

Williams, A. J. Small Business Failures in Australia: a Longitudinal Study' Unpub. Paper. The University of Newcastle, 1982.

Yarwood, A. T. *Asian Migration to Australia; The Background to Exclusion, 1896–23*, Parkville: Melbourne University Press 1964, p. 141.

Young, C., M. Petty & A. Faulkner, *Education and Employment of Turkish and Lebanese Youth*, Canberra: Commonwealth Department of Education, Australian Government Publishing Service, 1980.

Zuwiyya-Yamak, L. *The Syrian Social National Party*, Cambridge: Harvard University Press, 1966.

Newspaper Articles

Alison, Col 'Arab Australians in hostage mission' *The Sydney Morning Herald*, Friday 16 November 1990, p. 9.

'Court monitors circumcised girls', *The Sydney Morning Herald*, 1 March 1994, p. 2.

'The Lebanese law wears a moustache', *Monday Morning*, 24 February 1975, Beirut.

Hewett, Tony 'Muslims: law must recognise dower, *Sydney Morning Herald*, 25 September, 1991, p. 11; and 'Our laws upset love and marriage, Islam-style' *Sydney Morning Herald*, 26 September, 1991.

Obeid, Maha 'Australia the main target for Lebanese drug exports', *The Australian*, Tuesday 29 March 1994.

'Praying worker loses job' *The Sydney Morning Herald*, Friday17 April 1981.

'Iraq-Iran war leads to local Arab violence', *The Bulletin*, Tuesday 11 November 1980.

'Islamic world keeps an eye on Australian Moslems' in *The Financial Review*, Wednesday, 5 March 1980.

'Gulf war comes to Sydney suburbs', *The Sydney Morning Herald*, Tuesday 11 November 1980.

Solé, Robert 'Lifting a veil of fear from French schools', *Guardian Weekly*, 25 September 1994, p. 14.

Stewart, Cameron & Richard Jinman 'Violence tarnishes Macedonians;

Bolkus', *The Australia*, 12 April 1994, p. 4.
Woollacott, Martin 'The high political cost of morality campaigns', *Sydney Morning Herald*, 24th Jan 1994, p. 9.
Legal Cases
Haj v. Minister for Immigration & Ethnic Affairs, In the Federal Court of Australia, N. S. W. District Registry, General Division. Transcript No. G. 68 of 1981.
'The Council of the Municipality of Canterbury v. The Moslem Alawy Society Ltd. ' in the High Court of Australia, Sydney Office of the Registry No. 33 of 1985.

Index

Index